Models for Writing

Teacher's Book

5

Chris Buckton

Anne Sanderson

Series editor: Leonie Bennett

GINN

Author Team Chris Buckton
                  Anne Sanderson
Series editor: Leonie Bennett

                  Bill Ball (Scottish 5–14 Guidelines)
                  Robert Hunter (Northern Ireland Curriculum)
                  Beverley Parker and Steve Yates (ICT)

Ginn

Linacre House, Jordan Hill, Oxford, OX2 8DP
a division of Reed Educational and Professional Publishing Ltd
www.ginn.co.uk

Ginn is a registered trademark of Reed Educational and Professional Publishing Ltd

ISBN 0602 296897

04 03 02 01 00
10 9 8 7 6 5 4 3 2

Designed by Gecko Ltd, Bicester, Oxon
Cover designed by Gecko Ltd, Bicester, Oxon
Printed in the UK by Ashford Colour Press, Hampshire.

Contents

Introduction

Welcome to *Models for Writing*, the first complete programme to deliver Shared, Guided and Extended writing at Key Stage 2 in line with the requirements of the National Literacy Strategy framework. This programme links writing inside the Literacy Hour with extended writing outside the hour in a structured way. *Models for Writing* offers thorough coverage of the NLS writing objectives (*see matching chart on page 10*).

It also covers the requirements of the Scottish Guidelines on English Language 5 – 14 (1991), and the Northern Ireland Curriculum (1996) (*see correlation charts on pages 11 and 12*).

Improving Children's Writing

Models for Writing will help you to improve your pupils' writing across the ability range, bringing as many pupils as possible up to level 4 by the end of year 6.

It helps to improve writing through:

- stimulating model texts that interest and excite pupils
- modelled writing sessions which provide children with a clear structure
- differentiated activities and extended writing
- guided writing sessions that focus on both text and sentence level work.

Differentiation

Differentiation is offered in group and guided activities in the **Pupil's Book**. The activities are flagged with the following symbols:

> **1** Work for **lower attainers**, often supported by a photocopy master.
>
> **2** Work for the whole class. **Lower attainers** are often supported by a photocopy master such as a writing frame.
>
> **3** Work for **higher attainers**.

The lesson plans for each unit (*see pages 38–97*) offer specific guidance on how to work with different attaining groups during Guided writing.

Assessment

Models for Writing helps you to assess children's writing and judge how their skills are developing. You will find guidelines on assessment and annotated samples of children's writing at different levels on pages 22–31.

SAT Preparation

Suggestions for which units to use to practise writing under timed conditions are offered on pages 35–37.

Information and Communication Technology

Models for Writing includes a comprehensive section of ICT activities for each unit (*see pages 102–108*).

In the lesson plans, the **ICT** symbol indicates when an ICT activity could be used for that unit, and cross-references you to the appropriate page in the ICT section.

Structure/Components

Models for Writing has a simple structure which links Shared and Guided writing in the Literacy Hour with extended writing outside of the Hour.

Each Year of *Models for Writing* has:

Pupil's Book containing model texts, guided and supported activities, and extended writing.

Pupil's Book

Teacher's Book offering lesson plans for each unit, curriculum matching charts, assessment guidance, and ICT activities.

Teacher's Book

Overhead Transparencies of model texts and writing frames for whole class teaching.

Colour Overhead Transparancies

Photocopy Masters for differentiation and homework.

Photocopy Masters

How to use *Models for Writing*

When to Use *Models for Writing*

Each unit is designed around two lessons, with an additional extended writing session. You can use *Models for Writing* alongside any other literacy programme by slotting the two lessons into your planning. Alternatively, you could choose to spend more time on a particular unit or theme (*see 'Linked Units' below*) and extend the lessons over a whole week. Each unit focuses on a single writing objective, making it easy for you to see where they fit into your teaching, and making *Models for Writing* an extremely flexible programme.

How each unit works

Models for Writing is made up of 30 units. In each unit you will find:

LESSON ONE: MODEL TEXT

- The first lesson focuses on the study of a short model text from the **Pupil's Book**. (The text provides the model for the next lesson's writing.) Where annotation of the text is required, it is also offered on an OHT.

- Differentiated group activities are offered through the **Pupil's Book** and the **Photocopy Masters**.

LESSON TWO: WRITING

- *Shared Writing* – Shared or modelled writing based on the model text. Writing or planning frames are offered as OHTs where needed.

- *Guided, Group and Independent Writing* – Differentiated group and guided activities. Guidance is given on which group to work with during the Guided writing session.

EXTENDED WRITING

- Each unit ends with a suggested extended writing activity, to be completed outside of the lesson.

LINKED UNITS

- Some units are linked by topic or theme, or explore a particular skill at different levels. Opportunites for linking units are highlighted in the Planning Suggestion section of the lesson plan.

How to use *Models for Writing*

A *Models for Writing* Unit

 LESSON ONE

 LESSON TWO

Model Text

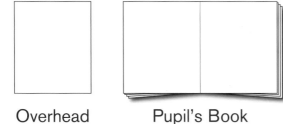

Overhead Transparencies

Pupil's Book

Shared Writing

Overhead Transparencies

Pupil's Book

Group Activities

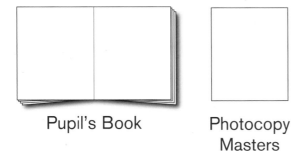

Pupil's Book

Photocopy Masters

Guided/Supported Writing

Pupil's Book

Photocopy Masters

Homework

Photocopy Masters

Extended Writing

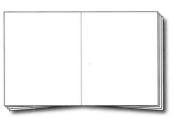

Pupil's Book

7

● How to use this *Teacher's Book*

unit number

unit heading

text type/ genre

main writing objective of unit with reference to NLS Framework

word and sentence level objectives

OHTs and PCMs needed are highlighted

suggestions for exploring the model text

differentiated group activities for the whole class

suggested homework activity

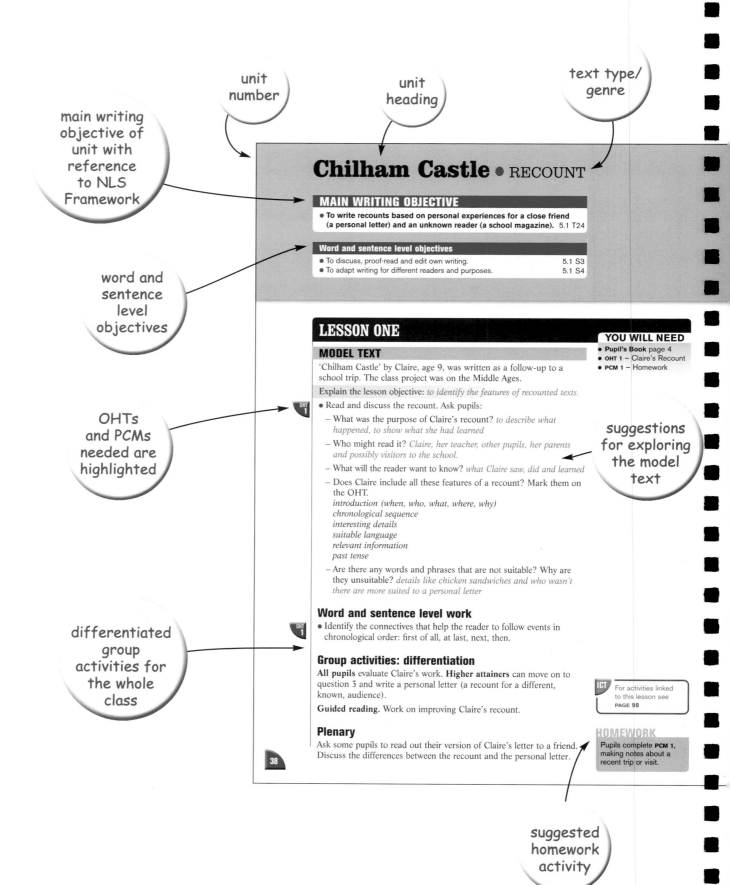

Chilham Castle ● RECOUNT

MAIN WRITING OBJECTIVE
● To write recounts based on personal experiences for a close friend (a personal letter) and an unknown reader (a school magazine). 5.1 T24

Word and sentence level objectives
● To discuss, proof-read and edit own writing. 5.1 S3
● To adapt writing for different readers and purposes. 5.1 S4

LESSON ONE

MODEL TEXT

YOU WILL NEED
● **Pupil's Book** page 4
● **OHT 1** – Claire's Recount
● **PCM 1** – Homework

'Chilham Castle' by Claire, age 9, was written as a follow-up to a school trip. The class project was on the Middle Ages.

Explain the lesson objective: *to identify the features of recounted texts.*

● Read and discuss the recount. Ask pupils:
  – What was the purpose of Claire's recount? *to describe what happened, to show what she had learned*
  – Who might read it? *Claire, her teacher, other pupils, her parents and possibly visitors to the school.*
  – What will the reader want to know? *what Claire saw, did and learned*
  – Does Claire include all these features of a recount? Mark them on the OHT.
  introduction (when, who, what, where, why)
  chronological sequence
  interesting details
  suitable language
  relevant information
  past tense
  – Are there any words and phrases that are not suitable? Why are they unsuitable? *details like chicken sandwiches and who wasn't there are more suited to a personal letter*

Word and sentence level work
● Identify the connectives that help the reader to follow events in chronological order: first of all, at last, next, then.

Group activities: differentiation
All pupils evaluate Claire's work. **Higher attainers** can move on to question 3 and write a personal letter (a recount for a different, known, audience).

Guided reading. Work on improving Claire's recount.

ICT For activities linked to this lesson see **PAGE 98**

Plenary
Ask some pupils to read out their version of Claire's letter to a friend. Discuss the differences between the recount and the personal letter.

HOMEWORK
Pupils complete **PCM 1**, making notes about a recent trip or visit.

38

links to reading objective from NLS Framework

referenced to Pupil's Book

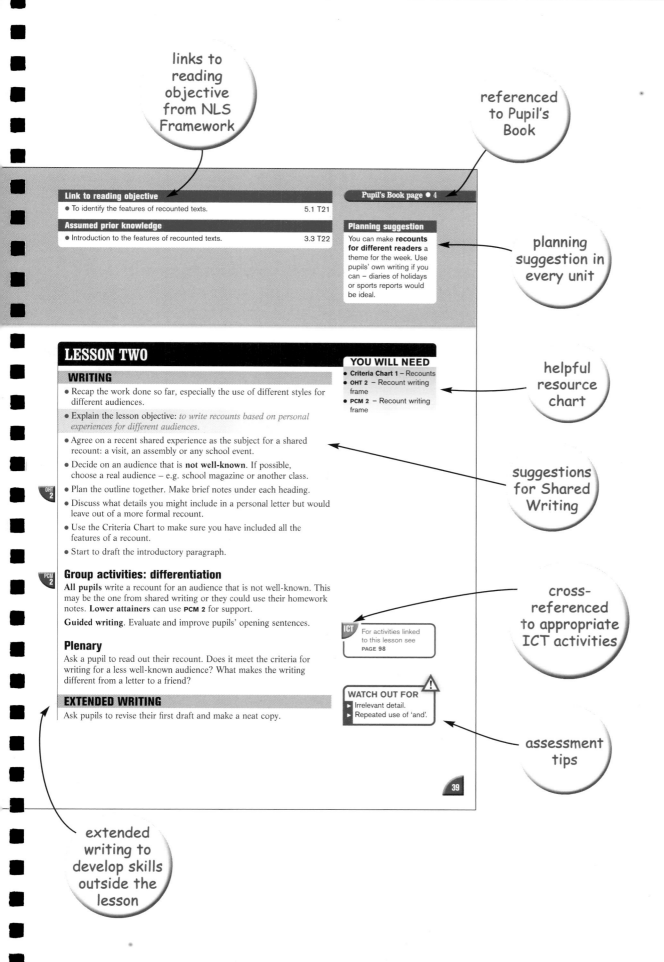

Link to reading objective	
● To identify the features of recounted texts.	5.1 T21

Assumed prior knowledge	
● Introduction to the features of recounted texts.	3.3 T22

Pupil's Book page ● 4

Planning suggestion

You can make **recounts for different readers** a theme for the week. Use pupils' own writing if you can – diaries of holidays or sports reports would be ideal.

planning suggestion in every unit

LESSON TWO

WRITING

- Recap the work done so far, especially the use of different styles for different audiences.
- Explain the lesson objective: *to write recounts based on personal experiences for different audiences.*
- Agree on a recent shared experience as the subject for a shared recount: a visit, an assembly or any school event.
- Decide on an audience that is **not well-known**. If possible, choose a real audience – e.g. school magazine or another class.
- Plan the outline together. Make brief notes under each heading.
- Discuss what details you might include in a personal letter but would leave out of a more formal recount.
- Use the Criteria Chart to make sure you have included all the features of a recount.
- Start to draft the introductory paragraph.

Group activities: differentiation

All pupils write a recount for an audience that is not well-known. This may be the one from shared writing or they could use their homework notes. **Lower attainers** can use **PCM 2** for support.

Guided writing. Evaluate and improve pupils' opening sentences.

Plenary

Ask a pupil to read out their recount. Does it meet the criteria for writing for a less well-known audience? What makes the writing different from a letter to a friend?

EXTENDED WRITING

Ask pupils to revise their first draft and make a neat copy.

YOU WILL NEED
- **Criteria Chart 1** – Recounts
- **OHT 2** – Recount writing frame
- **PCM 2** – Recount writing frame

helpful resource chart

suggestions for Shared Writing

ICT For activities linked to this lesson see **PAGE 98**

WATCH OUT FOR
▶ Irrelevant detail.
▶ Repeated use of 'and'.

cross-referenced to appropriate ICT activities

assessment tips

39

extended writing to develop skills outside the lesson

NLS Writing Objectives Matching Chart

Unit key

Unit 1	Chilham Castle	Unit 16	An Odd Kettle of Fish
Unit 2	Reading Logs	Unit 17	Lord Krishna's Flute
Unit 3	Kimball's Green	Unit 18	The Blue Whale
Unit 4	Concrete Poems	Unit 19	From Ice to Water
Unit 5	The Angel of Nitshill Road	Unit 20	Mountain Bikes
Unit 6	Working Children	Unit 21	Feathered Friends
Unit 7	People Poems	Unit 22	Gran can you Rap?
Unit 8	Grab the Reader	Unit 23	The Snargets
Unit 9	Paper Planes	Unit 24	Leave your car at home
Unit 10	Morpurgo Interview	Unit 25	Book Report
Unit 11	Morpurgo Manuscript	Unit 26	Too Little, Too Late
Unit 12	Then and Now	Unit 27	Agony Aunts
Unit 13	Banana-Day Trip	Unit 28	Child Labour
Unit 14	Krakus and the Dragon	Unit 29	Hunt the Baby
Unit 15	Raggle Taggle Gypsies	Unit 30	No Smoking!

MAIN WRITING OBJECTIVE

	Main Writing Objective	Units matched
Term 1 – Fiction		
S3	To discuss and edit their own writing	Unit 2
T11	To experiment with alternative story openings	Unit 8, Unit 11, Unit 13
T13	To record ideas, reflections and predictions about a book	Unit 3, Unit 10
T14	To map out texts showing development and structure	Unit 5
T15	To write new scenes or characters into a story; to write in the manner of the writer, using paragraphs to organise	Unit 3, Unit 5
T16	To convey feelings and moods in poetry	Unit 4, Unit 7
T17	To write metaphors	Unit 6, Unit 7
T18	To write own playscript including production notes	
T19	To annotate a playscript for performance	
Term 1 – Non-fiction		
T24	To write recounts for known and unknown readers	Unit 1, Unit 12
T25	To write instructional texts and test them out	Unit 9
T26	To make notes for different purposes	Unit 10, Unit 12
T27	To use simple abbreviations in note-taking	Unit 12
Term 2 – Fiction		
T11	To write own versions of legends, myths and fables	Unit 14, Unit 15, Unit 16, Unit 17
T12	To write extensions of poems, adding verses or substituting own words	Unit 15, Unit 16
T13	To review and edit writing to produce a final form	Unit 12
Term 2 – Non-fiction		
T21	To convert personal notes into notes for others to read	Unit 18, Unit 19
T22	To write short non-chronological reports and explanatory texts	Unit 19, Unit 20, Unit 21
T23	To record and acknowledge sources in own writing	Unit 19, Unit 20
T24	To evaluate their own writing	
Term 3 – Fiction		
T7	To write from another character's point of view	
T8	To record predictions and reflections while reading	Unit 23
T9	To write in the style of an author	Unit 29
T10	To write discursively about a novel or story	Unit 25
T11	To use performance poems as models to write poetry	Unit 22
Term 3 – Non-fiction		
T17	To draft and write letters for real purposes	Unit 27, Unit 28
T18	To set out and justify a point of view; to write a persuasive news editorial /leaflet	Unit 24, Unit 26, Unit 30
T19	To construct a persuasive argument	Unit 24, Unit 26, Unit 30

Scottish 5–14 Curriculum Guideline Levels

STRAND	LEVEL C	UNITS	LEVEL D	UNITS
Functional Writing	**Write in an appropriate form and with adequate vocabulary to communicate key events, facts or ideas.** • use other contexts e.g. Environment Studies • purpose and audience should be established • note-taking with teacher help – from TV etc with reports built from these • teacher helps pupils analyse texts e.g. reading material to extract important data	1 9 12 20 17 18	**Write in a variety of forms to communicate key events, facts or ideas using appropriate organisation and vocabulary. By reading and discussing texts with teachers, pupils will identify main forms of functional writing and use them appropriately.** • write succinctly as appropriate • explore appropriate use of notes, lists and diagrams	2 26 4 25 9 27 12 28 19 29 21
Personal Writing	**Write about a personal experience for a specific purpose and audience using appropriate organisation and vocabulary.** • the sense of purpose and audience will be developed for each type of writing • appropriate contexts used	1 2 3 11 14	**Write about personal experiences expressing thoughts and feelings for a specific purpose and audience using appropriate organisation and vocabulary.** • using common situations begin to depict emotions in writing • shared writing on board with group to model effective styles • look at appropriate style for audience and purpose	14 29 18 26 25 27 28
Imaginative Writing	**Write a brief imaginative story, poem or play using appropriate organisation and vocabulary.** • teacher will provide stimulating contexts for imaginative writing • teacher draws attention to character, scene, setting and action • pupils begin to look at events from the point of view of different characters • poetry developed to include reading aloud own and other's work	3 15 4 22 5 8 10 13 14	**Write imaginative pieces in various genres using appropriate organisation and vocabulary.** • look at how to turn stories into playscripts etc • tell a story in role – newsreader etc • look at first and third person narratives in reading material and past and present tense – begin to use	6 8 15 19 16 23 29
Punctuation and Structure	**In the writing tasks listed, punctuate many sentences accurately including simple use of commas and question marks; begin to use paragraphs to structure writing.** • teacher still models use of the above and encourages pupils to use them in own writing • co-operative writing can be used to aid group discussion, reinforce sense of audience and motivate re-drafting skills	3 7 8 11 13	**In the writing tasks listed, punctuate most sentences accurately; achieve some variety in sentence structure, use paragraphs and begin to indicate speech marks in some way where appropriate.** • use paragraphs to separate aspects of a story • use good models to show how sentence structure can create atmosphere, mood and aid meaning • look at a variety of texts for different ways of representing speech – scripts, comics etc	4 15 5 19 10 28 11 12
Knowledge About Language	**Pupils show that they know, understand and can use at least the following terms – noun, verb, comma, question mark, purpose, audience.** • the teacher will continue to model these through class novels etc and encourage pupils to ensure they use all these conventions in their own work	1 8 11 14 22	**Pupils show that they know, understand and can use at least the following terms – vowel and consonant, adjective, adverb, pronoun and conjunction, masculine and feminine, singular and plural, tense, paragraph.** • the teacher will introduce the above through contexts and models as well as individual teaching lessons	3 19 5 21 11 25 13 29 14 17

The strands for Spelling and Handwriting and Presentation would be covered by the teacher differentiating according to each pupil's ability.

Models for Writing and the Northern Ireland Curriculum

UNIT	LEVEL
1	4
2	4
3	4
4	4
5	4/5
6	4
7	4/5
8	4
9	4
10	4/5
11	4/5
12	4/5
13	4
14	4/5
15	4
16	4/5
17	4
18	4
19	4
20	4/5
21	4
22	4
23	4/5
24	4/5
25	4
26	4/5
27	4/5
28	4/5
29	4
30	4/5

Opportunities are provided for:

WRITING

- Modelled writing
- Shared writing
- Teaching planning, drafting, revising, proof-reading, editing and publishing in a structured way
- Collaborative work
- Children to see their teacher write
- Extending vocabulary
- Writing in a range of forms
- Writers to show an awareness of audience
- Writing for a range of audiences
- Increasing proficiency in the use of syntax and punctuation
- Discussion with the teacher
- Discussion with other pupils
- Gathering and organising ideas
- Making notes
- Writing in a range of types
- Using a problem solving approach to analysing texts
- Responding to reading
- Experimenting with rhymes, rhythms, verbal play and dialect
- Appreciating some of the differences between spoken and written language
- Differentiated responses

READING

- Reading aloud
- Recognising and expressing explicit and some implicit meanings and attitudes in a range of texts
- Becoming aware of the writer's intentions and use of language and structure
- Supporting a response with reference to text
- Read about people from other cultures, religion, race or social background
- Reading for a variety of purposes
- Engaging with a range of texts
- Shared reading
- Modelled reading
- Independent reading
- Discussing features of language
- Modelling writing on forms encountered in reading

TALKING and LISTENING

- Engaging in formal and informal discussion
- Interacting with other pupils
- Interacting with a range of audiences
- Talking and listening for a range of purposes
- Listening and responding to a range of texts
- Exploring dialect
- Expressing and justifying opinions
- Preparing and presenting oral presentations

About Shared Writing

In Shared Writing, you, the 'expert writer', model the writing process. Pupils should contribute ideas, calling on their experience of exploring the model text, and you develop them further.

Before Writing

Talk with the pupils about:

- the text type and its features ●
- the purpose and audience ●
- the structure, and how best to order the events or information
- the layout – length, illustration and final presentation
- possible ways of planning – brainstorming, story boards, writing ● frames etc.

> What do we know about texts like these?

> Who are we writing for?

> How can we organise our ideas?

During Shared Writing

- where appropriate, display the annotated model text so the class can refer to it
- explain exactly what you like or do not like about the ideas the pupils offer
- demonstrate how to share ideas and work collaboratively
- 'think aloud' as you write so that pupils understand how to ● consider different options
- demonstrate how writers work at each stage of composition
- show pupils how to apply the conventions of written English – focus on specific aspects of punctuation or spelling
- demonstrate how to revise the writing by re-reading and making changes
- keep the writing short.

> I'm making this into a longer sentence by adding extra detail.

After Writing

Show pupils how to:

- talk about their writing; introduce the vocabulary they will need
- edit and redraft their work, perhaps moving larger chunks of text ● as well as adding and deleting words and phrases
- make the link again between reading and writing, considering their work as a reader would – What does it make you feel? What is left ● out or not clear?
- proof-read, checking for sense as well as spelling and punctuation errors
- prepare for final presentation.

> Let's add an adjective to describe what he looks like. How should we describe him?

> Does this sound right? Is it better if we take out these words

REMEMBER

Do

- share the lesson objective with the pupils
- emphasise purpose and audience
- refer back to the model text
- direct and control the Shared Writing
- encourage pupils to contribute at their own level
- build on pupils' suggestions
- write with pupils whenever possible
- 'think aloud' as you are writing
- encourage pupils to revise as they write
- teach self-help techniques
- expect pupils to proof-read and edit their work

Don't

- offer unfocused praise
- be afraid to make specific criticisms
- try to correct every aspect of their writing

About Guided Writing

Guided Writing is about providing support for children during the writing process.

For Guided Writing, children should be in small groups according to writing ability. You may teach specific skills, or dip in and out of writing with the pupils, discussing as you go. Providing support while children are working is especially important.

Offer guidance throughout the writing process. On pages 16–19 you will find prompt charts to help you guide pupils through each stage of composition.

Before Writing

Help pupils to prepare by:

- reviewing the task ●

- collecting ideas – maybe by brainstorming or spider webbing

- talking about how to organise the material – choosing key ideas, grouping them, putting them in the best order, working out how to link them

- jotting down words and phrases that might be useful

- checking for gaps in their plan.

> Who are we writing for?

> How shall we group all our ideas?

During Writing

Join the group when they are already writing. Observe for a while, then:

- find out how it is going and identify any problems

- focus on specific elements of composition, just a few sentences at a time ●

- remind pupils of the model text and the work done in Shared Writing

- help to develop ideas and build confidence ●

- use appropriate terminology.

> What could we add to give us more detail?

> That's a really good connective because...

After Writing

Respond to pupils' work by:

- finding out what the writers were trying to achieve ●

- reviewing the task and recapping the features of the text type

- asking writers to read out sections they are pleased with

- giving precise, positive feedback which lets writers know what effect their writing has had on a reader ●

- asking writers to identify the parts which need development

- encouraging suggestions for improvement.

> What are we looking for in this text?

> I liked the bit when...

Teaching sequence for Guided Writing when planning written work

STEPS	TYPICAL CUES
Review	• What do we know about writing texts like this? • What is the job in hand? • How shall we go about it?
Gather ideas	• What do we want to say? • What ideas do we have?
Marshal the material (select – shape– sequence)	• Which ideas shall we use? • How can we group ideas together? • What order should we put them in? • How can we link the ideas together?
Gather support	• What details can we add? • How can we explain or expand? • What evidence can we give? • What words and expressions come to mind?
Rehearse	• Does it look right? • What are the gaps? • How could we start? • How can it be improved?

Teaching sequence for Guided Writing when pupils are drafting

STEPS	TYPICAL CUES
Review	• What's the task in hand? • What do we know already? • What are the main features of this kind of text? • How did the author in yesterday's Shared Reading tackle this?
Cue in	• How might you start? • Let me start you off . . . • Let's try starting with action this time.
Try it	• Identification • Exploration/generalisation • Addition/deletion/substitution • Praise/building confidence • Assessment • Use of terminology/reflection • Extension/development • Drawing writing into talk
Recapitulate	• What worked? • What helped? • What can we use again?

Teaching sequence for Guided Writing when responding to written work

STEPS	TYPICAL CUES
Recapitulate	• What are we looking for in this piece of writing? • What are the main features of this kind of text?
Read and reward	• What I liked about this was . . . • That makes me wonder . . . • I noticed . . . • Where are the best moments?
Compare and generalise	• Who else tried it that way? • What other ways have been used? • Which of these worked well? • Which tends to work best?
Isolate weakness	• Where are the false notes? • Why does it not quite work? • Which is the hardest part to get right? • What could be improved?
Support improvement	• How could you deal with the problem? • Could we say . . .? • You could try . . . • Start like this . . . • Try writing that part again . . .

Teaching activities: intervening in the writing process

1 Identification/Selection of important features	What I noticed/liked about this was . . . because . . .
2 Addition Deletion Substitution	What can we add? What can we leave out/get rid of? What else can we put in there to make it better?
3 Exploration/Generalisation	The reason why . . . It's useful to know that . . . What tends to work best is . . . because . . . The rule/pattern for this is . . . When else does this happen?
4 Praise/Building confidence	I really like the way you . . . because . . . I really like . . . because . . . That works well because . . .
5 Assessment Assessing strengths, weaknesses Correction	Which parts work best? Why does it not quite work? Which is the hardest part to get right?
6 Use of terminology/Reflection	I really like the term you chose because . . . Which term could you use here?
7 Extension/Development	Could we use, say . . .? You could try . . . You can carry on by . . .
8 Drawing writing into talking	Tell me how you would write . . . So you think that . . . What do you think about . . .? Say a little more about . . .

Independent and Extended Writing

Independent Writing

Independent writing activities flow directly from Shared or Guided writing. In independent group activities, pupils are still supported by working collaboratively and by using writing frames. **Writing frames can be a powerful support for writers but they can also become a straightjacket. It is very important to show pupils how to adapt them and how to generate their own**. Support also comes from exploring the model text, the preparatory work completed for homework and the Shared Writing session.

Models for Writing also provides **Prompt Charts** which list the main features of each text type or writing process, and these can be displayed for pupils to refer to. (The Prompt Charts are located at the back of the **Photocopy Masters** folder.)

Extended Writing

The suggestions for extended writing in *Models for Writing* encourage pupils to carry on with their writing outside the Literacy Hour; to discuss and revise their work; to take their work to presentation standard and, where appropriate, to publish it using ICT. The lesson plans that accompany each unit offer suggestions for how you might integrate the units and the extended writing activities into your weekly planning.

Models for Writing emphasises that writing for different purposes requires different approaches. A shopping list or a quick note will not require redrafting, but a brochure about the school, or a web site, might take several sessions to complete.

Pair and Collaborative Writing: Response Partners

Models for Writing offers pupils ample opportunity to talk about their work and to help each other by giving feedback, as well as times when they can write in near silence. Their feedback will be most effective if they are given guidance and practice in reading each other's work and giving advice on it. Encourage them to act as response partners on a regular basis.

At first their comments may be superficial. They need to learn to:

- find out what the writer is trying to do
- pay attention to content
- identify which features to comment on
- balance positive and negative comments
- be constructive.

On pages 32–34 you will find **Self-Assessment** sheets to support this process. Discuss and model the process in Shared and Guided Writing.

Assessing Children's Writing: how to improve your pupils' work

Knowing it is good or bad is not good enough!

To reach literacy targets, we need to know *precisely* what pupils need to improve upon. What are the features in pupil X's writing that make him so fluent? What *exactly* are the difficulties that pupil Y is having which may prevent her reaching level 4 by the end of Key Stage 2? If you can diagnose the symptoms you are on the way to finding a cure. Through careful assessment and specific feedback, you and your pupils will find out what they can do already and what they need to do next. On the basis of this you can plan future tasks to take their learning forward. The most helpful assessments focus on a few specific features. Too much information can be overwhelming and de-motivating.

If the learning objective is clear and precise then assessment is easy. Much of the assessment occurs with the pupil during writing, particularly in guided group work. Talking together helps you to find out what the writer is trying to do and what difficulties they are encountering.

Pupils can also get feedback for themselves. Make sure they know the purpose of every writing task and the criteria for assessing it. Show them how to assess their own writing against the criteria and how to work effectively with a response partner.

Prompt Charts

To check whether the piece of writing has the appropriate structure and features for its 'genre' or 'text type', use the Prompt Charts at the back of the **Photocopy Masters** folder.

You can also give these charts to pupils to help them remember the criteria, and structure their writing accordingly.

Self-Assessment

Ask pupils to use **Photocopy Master** A (*see page 32*) to assist their work with a response partner. They can also use **Photocopy Master** B (*see page 33*) for support with their editing, and **Photocopy Master** C (*see page 34*) to assess their own work.

Help them to develop the habit of reflecting on their own writing. If they are involved in setting their own targets they will be much more motivated to achieve them.

Questions to Consider

Purpose and audience

- Is the form of the writing suitable for its purpose?
- Is the writer aware of the reader?
- Does the writing engage the reader's interest?

Structure and organisation

- How effective are the opening and ending?
- How well does the writer organise ideas?
- Does the structure reflect the features of the text type?
- Is sentence construction varied?
- Are sentences and paragraphs joined with a variety of connectives?

Grammar and style

- Is the writing grammatically correct?
- Is punctuation used correctly?
- Are verb tenses consistent?
- Is there unnecessary repetition?
- Does the writing flow?
- Is it coherent?
- Is the vocabulary well chosen?

Presentation

- Is handwriting or word processing clear and suitable for the purpose?
- Is the presentation appropriate?

Spelling

- Is spelling usually accurate?
- Does spelling show knowledge of word derivation, common patterns, and prefixes/suffixes?
- Are guesses plausible?

Fiction: Telephone conversation
Achievements: Level 3
Purpose and audience:
NLS 5.3 T9   To write in the style of the author, e.g. writing additional dialogue.
NLS 5.3 T19 Persuasive writing.

Summary

The form of the writing reflects conversational telephone tone but does not develop character or capture author's style. It would have been better as an oral task with group audience. The writer has not made enough use of text or of persuasive language – maybe the task was not made clear, especially the 'persuasion' element.

The writing is generally too bare to engage the reader's interest.

Structure and Organisation

• Clearly organised with appropriate opening and ending.

• Ideas organised logically but not developed.

• Knowledge of telephone language e.g. incomplete sentences/colloquial phrases.

Grammar and Style

• Grammatically correct and correctly punctuated, consistent use of colons – though no use of commas.

• Verb tenses consistent, but does not flow and does not capture the text style.

Presentation

• Carefully laid out; regular, fluent handwriting.

Spelling

• Accurate spelling of common polysyllabic words (favour, tomorrow).

What next?

• Oral tasks to develop ideas further and to collect persuasive devices.

• More work on dialogue and behaviour in *Charlotte's Web*, picking out characteristic words and phrases.

• In future break tasks down into separate parts – too much attempted here.

• Investigate use of commas.

Telephone Conversation – Fern and Mr Zuckerman

Conversation focus: Fern is trying to persuade Mr Zuckerman to take the pig (Wilbur).

Fern: Hello Uncle Homer is that you?

Mr Z: Yes why?

Fern: Can you do me a little favour?

Mr. Z: Yes what is it?

Fern: Can you look after my pig for me please?

Mr. Z: How old is he?

Fern: just a baby.

Mr. Z: ok. when are you bringing him?

Fern: Tomorrow.

Mr. Z: ok. and I'll feed him slops every day.

Fern: thanks bye.

charlotte's Web.

Fiction: Hiding Horror!
Achievements: Level 4
Purpose and audience:
NLS 5.3 S2   To adapt writing for different audiences and purposes – a class newspaper based on Berlie Doherty's *Children of Winter.*

Summary

The writer understood how to tackle the task, used an appropriate form of writing, and was motivated. The writer also changed the tone to suit a newspaper audience and engaged the reader's interest.

Structure and Organisation

- A fair attempt at a difficult text type – few children read newspapers. Some knowledge of key features e.g. catchy alliterative headline, reporter's name, use of indirect and direct speech, emotive journalistic tone; but some gaps e.g. reason is not made clear soon enough.

- Shows some grasp of characters' viewpoints.

- Summary of basic story is well organised and dramatic; punchy opening and ending.

- Varied sentence construction e.g. passive voice, embedded noun phrase.

- Some use of connectives: but, then, and with that.

- Good use of dialogue to tell story.

Grammar and Style

- Grammatically correct apart from use of 'us'.

- Punctuation correct – good use of commas and semi-colon.

- Verb tenses accurate, moving between present and past.

- Flows well and is coherent apart from 'board' at end.

- Vocabulary chosen to reflect journalistic style.

Presentation

- Some knowledge of newspaper conventions but not sure about column layout.

Spelling

- Spelling mostly accurate apart from inresponsable (shows some knowledge of possible prefixes and suffixes) and plauge (reversal shows gap in phoneme knowledge).

What next?

- More investigation of news story layout and structure – 'who what where why when' analysis.

- For writing, use DTP with newspaper format. Try a more accessible medium – e.g. TV interview.

- Look at journalistic use of adjective phrases in describing characters.

- Word level: investigate -ible and -able.

Hiding Horror!

14th November

report by Hazel Smith.

A barn has been found with three children in it named Dan, Catherine and Tessa. They say that their mother left them to give them a chance to live, but personally us reporters think she is an irresponsible mother. We asked the oldest child, Catherine, aged fifteen, what life was like in the barn. Her reply was; "Well it's better than having the plague", but they need more warmth, food and a lot more attention. Dan, aged seven, shouted out; "We've had to patch up the walls." Tessa, aged twelve, said quietly, "Catherine has been very good to us." Catherine then said, "please leave; you might have the plague." And with that she pushed us out and shut the barn.

Non-fiction: Dear Mr Price
Achievements: Level 3
Purpose and audience:
NLS 5.3 T17 To draft and write individual letters for real purposes.

Summary
The writer has understood the purpose well and produced a real letter, but they are only partially aware of what the reader needs to know. The letter engages interest because it conveys real feelings.

Structure and Organisation
- Logical structure organised into paragraphs but ideas not extended – lack of detail.
- Understands letter writing conventions.

Grammar and Style
- Grammatically correct. Punctuation marks sentences; correct use of capitals, but commas incorrectly placed.
- Verb tenses consistent.
- Does not flow because argument is not developed. Lack of explanation makes it seem a little incoherent.

Presentation
- Handwriting clear and legible, deliberately not joined for this particular task.

Spelling
- Accurate spelling including common polysyllabic words (parents, sincerely, behalf).

What next?
- A Shared Reading session using a model letter to illustrate the use of detail and persuasive devices.
- More oral work to extend ideas and brainstorming notes before writing.
- Work on commas – practise reading aloud with pauses.

Dear Mr Price

We have very few wild life places in the city and, we have worked so hard on the wasteland.
I hope you will let us have it because we have all helped the, wasteland, and the parents have helped us too.

Yours
Sincerely
Simon
Hussey
on behalf of the
School

Non-fiction: Obstacle Netball
Achievements: Level 4
Purpose and audience:
NLS 5.1 T25 To write instructions and test them out.

Summary

The writer has a confident grasp of the task and awareness of audience. They know how to apply the features of instructional texts. The tone is lively and direct and effectively engages the reader.

Structure and Organisation

- Well-structured – e.g. listing equipment, sequential stages. Good opening (object of the game), but needs re-positioning; very effective ending.
- All the features of the text type are here – clear headings, bullet points. The 'How to Play' section could include more detail about the markers.
- Diagrams not easy to interpret.

Grammar and Style

- Uses imperative verbs.
- Clearly punctuated including use of stem with colon ('Did you:') but NB capitals unnecessary.
- Flows easily.

Presentation

- Well presented. Alot of thought has been given to the layout although the diagrams are a bit small. Could benefit from showing a close up of the skittle and cane.
- Handwriting is fluent. Letter 'j' incorrectly placed.

Spelling

- Accurate spelling throughout.

What next?

- Test out the instructions to see if there is enough detail about setting out the game.
- Work on diagrams/labelling.
- Handwriting – 'j' descender.

obstacle netball

~~for teams of 2-5 players~~

Equipment
♦ 20 markers
♦ 8 Skittles
♦ 4 canes
♦ 2 balls

Getting ready
♦ Set out the Skittles and markers as shown below:

♦ Balance the canes on the Skittles at the third hole up.

♦ Divide into equal teams.

Object of the game
To be the first team to finish the course.

Try this to warm up:

How to play
♦ Start at opposite ends of the course.
♦ Bounce the ball round the course
♦ When you shoot a goal, run and fetch the ball. You are then the goal keeper.
♦ you repeat this. The first team to finish wins.

Did you:
♦ Congratulate the other team when they won?
Enjoy the game?
Work well together?

Happy playing!

Working with a response partner

Read your work aloud.

Is it interesting/enjoyable?

Is anything not clear? List below.

-
-
-

Is anything missing? List below.

-
-
-

Can you suggest:

- alternative words or expressions?

- a better beginning or ending?

Is it too long or too short?

Can anything be cut? If so, what?

Has the writer done what he or she was asked to do?

Editing check-list

Remember to check:	checked ✓
Are there enough details to help the reader?	☐
Have you used capital letters and punctuation?	☐
Is speech set out correctly?	☐
Do all verbs and nouns agree?	☐
Are all spellings correct?	☐
Are there any repeated phrases or unneccessary words that you can take out?	☐

Self-assessment

Title of writing: _____

What was the task? _____

_____

_____

How difficult was it? (Circle the score out of 10)

1   2   3   4   5   6   7   8   9   10

How happy are you with it? (Circle the score out of 10)

1   2   3   4   5   6   7   8   9   10

What do you think you have done well?

_____

_____

What didn't work?

_____

_____

What did your response partner say about it?

_____

_____

Do you agree?

_____

What is your new target?

_____

_____

The six pieces of writing below can be set under timed conditions. It is a good idea to set one piece of timed writing every half term. Give the pupils 15 minutes to plan the task and 45 minutes to complete their writing.

Unit 3 The Dark Streets of Kimball's Green

TASK: To write a description of what happens next. What happens when Mrs Vaughan comes back?

Assessment Criteria

Purpose and organisation

- Does the story engage the reader's interest?
- Is characterisation evident through description, and direct and reported speech?
- Are the paragraphs detailed, clear and correct?
- Is the story well organised, with a clear beginning, middle and end?

Grammar and style

- Is it written in the style of the author?
- How is language used to give information about characters: adverbs and adjectives?
- Use of synonyms?
- Correct use of dialogue?
- Punctuation and verb tenses consistent?

Unit 13 Banana-Day Trip

TASK: To write a short recount of something that happened to you when you were younger.
You should:
- focus on one particular incident
- use interesting details to paint a vivid picture of character and setting.

Assessment Criteria

Purpose and organisation

- Is the recount coherent, with a clear beginning, middle and end?
- Is characterisation evident through direct and reported speech?
- Does the writing seek to interest the reader?

Grammar and style

- Are sentences correctly indicated by full stops, capital letters and question marks?
- Is speech set out correctly?
- Does it include interesting use of adverbs and adjectives?

Unit 19 From Ice to Water

TASK: To write a short explanatory text.
(This could be linked to the subject matter covered in Shared Writing.)

Assessment Criteria

Purpose and organisation

- Is the form of writing suitable for the purpose?
- Is there a short introductory statement that tells us what the explanation is about?
- Does the writing explain what happens and why?
- Does the writing follow a logical sequence?
- Has thought been given to layout and use of diagrams?

Grammar and style

Does the writing use:

- time connectives?
- causal connectives?
- impersonal language?
- present tense?

Unit 21 Feathered Friends

TASK: To write a non-chronological, impersonal report about a subject you know well.

Assessment Criteria

Purpose and organisation

- Is the form of writing suitable for the purpose and audience?
- Is there a short opening paragraph that introduces the subject?
- Is the report concise?
- Are related facts grouped in paragraphs?

Grammar and style

Does the writing use:

- formal language?
- impersonal pronouns?
- mainly present tense?
- facts not opinions?

Unit 28 Child Labour

TASK: To write a protest letter to a newspaper about a subject you feel strongly about.

Assessment Criteria

Purpose and organisation

- Is the writing suitable for audience and purpose?
- Does the writing have a logical structure, e.g. an opening statement and a summary that repeats the key points?
- Is there a persuasive argument throughout the letter?
- Is the argument clear?

Grammar and style

- Are letter writing conventions used accurately?
- Does the letter pose questions?
- Are sentences correctly demarcated by full stops, capital letters and question marks?

Unit 30 No Smoking!

TASK: To write a leaflet encouraging children to stop eating junk food. Remember that the leaflet is aiming to **persuade** people.

Assessment Criteria

Purpose and organisation

- Is the writing suitable for the purpose?
- Is there an awareness of design and layout?
- Are points logically ordered?
- Is the writing persuasive?

Grammar and style

- Are bullet points, headings and sub-headings used?
- Are sentences properly demarcated by full stops, capital letters and question marks?

Chilham Castle • RECOUNT

MAIN WRITING OBJECTIVE

- **To write recounts based on personal experiences for a close friend (a personal letter) and an unknown reader (a school magazine).** 5.1 T24

Word and sentence level objectives

- To discuss, proof-read and edit own writing.   5.1 S3
- To adapt writing for different readers and purposes.   5.1 S4

LESSON ONE

YOU WILL NEED

- **Pupil's Book** page 4
- **OHT 1** – Claire's Recount
- **PCM 1** – Homework

MODEL TEXT

'Chilham Castle' by Claire, age 9, was written as a follow-up to a school trip. The class project was on the Middle Ages.

Explain the lesson objective: *to identify the features of recounted texts.*

- Read and discuss the recount. Ask pupils:

  – What was the purpose of Claire's recount? *to describe what happened, to show what she had learned*

  – Who might read it? *Claire, her teacher, other pupils, her parents and possibly visitors to the school.*

  – What will the reader want to know? *what Claire saw, did and learned*

  – Does Claire include all these features of a recount? Mark them on the OHT.
    introduction (when, who, what, where, why)
    chronological sequence + connectives
    interesting details
    suitable language
    relevant information
    past tense

  – Are there any words and phrases that are not suitable? Why are they unsuitable? *details like chicken sandwiches and who wasn't there are more suited to a personal letter*

Word and sentence level work

- Identify the connectives that help the reader to follow events in chronological order: *first of all, at last, next, then.*

Group activities: differentiation

All pupils evaluate Claire's work. **Higher attainers** can move on to question 3 and write a personal letter (a recount for a different, known, audience).

Guided reading. Work on improving Claire's recount.

Plenary

Ask some pupils to read out their version of Claire's letter to a friend. Discuss the differences between the recount and the personal letter.

ICT For activities linked to this lesson see **PAGE 102**

HOMEWORK
Pupils complete **PCM 1**, making notes about a recent trip or visit.

Link to reading objective

- To identify the features of recounted texts. 5.1 T21

Assumed prior knowledge

- Introduction to the features of recounted texts. 3.3 T22

Planning suggestion

You can make **recounts for different readers** a theme for the week. Use pupils' own writing if you can – diaries of holidays or sports reports would be ideal.

LESSON TWO

WRITING

- Recap the work done so far, especially the use of different styles for different audiences.
- Explain the lesson objective: *to write recounts based on personal experiences for different audiences.*
- Agree on a recent shared experience as the subject for a shared recount: a visit, an assembly or any school event.
- Decide on an audience that is **not well-known**. If possible, choose a real audience – e.g. school magazine or another class.
- Plan the outline together. Make brief notes under each heading.
- Discuss what details you might include in a personal letter but would leave out of a more formal recount.
- Use the **Prompt Chart** to make sure you have included all the features of a recount.
- Start to draft the introductory paragraph.

Group activities: differentiation

All pupils write a recount for an audience that is not well-known. This may be the one from shared writing or they could use their homework notes. **Lower attainers** can use PCM 2 for support.

Guided writing. Evaluate and improve pupils' opening sentences.

Plenary

Ask a pupil to read out their recount. Does it meet the criteria for writing for a less well-known audience? What makes the writing different from a letter to a friend?

EXTENDED WRITING

Ask pupils to revise their first draft and make a neat copy.

YOU WILL NEED

- **Prompt Chart 1** – Recounts
- **OHT 2** – Recount writing frame
- **PCM 2** – Recount writing frame

ICT For activities linked to this lesson see **PAGE 102**

WATCH OUT FOR
- ► Irrelevant detail.
- ► Repeated use of 'and'.

2

Reading Logs • RECORDING IDEAS

MAIN WRITING OBJECTIVE
- **To record ideas and reflections.**   5.1 T13

Word and sentence level objectives
- To adapt writing for different purposes.   5.1 S4
- To collect idiomatic phrases.   5.1 W9

LESSON ONE

YOU WILL NEED
- **Pupil's Book** pages 6–7
- **PCM 3** – Homework

MODEL TEXT

- Introduce the idea of reading logs. Explain that they are like diaries for recording feelings and ideas about what you are reading. They log a journey of exploration through your mind. They are different from book reviews because you write them for yourself.

- Explain the lesson objective: *to look at some examples of reading logs.*

- Explain that there are different ways of writing reading logs.

- **PB** Read 'Everything I read yesterday' (Peter's List). Explain that this reading log is in note form. Why do pupils think Peter made his list? *To see how much reading he did and to find out how many different kinds of reading there are.*

- Read the extract from Beth's 'Reading log'. It describes Beth's changing thoughts and feelings as she starts reading a new book. Ask pupils:

  – What ideas was Beth trying to sort out? *what's going on in the book; exploring how she feels about it*

  – What does she want to find out next? *why the girl is on her own*

  – Can you find any places in both logs where the writing is in note form? *all of Peter's list; several examples on first page of Beth's log*

Word and sentence level work

PB 1 Discuss which words Beth has left out. Ask pupils why they think she has done this.

2 Pick out idiomatic words and phrases: *a bit weird; complete muddle; the creeps.* Are they suitable here? *quite appropriate because they describe her feelings and it is informal writing*

Group activities: differentiation
All pupils answer both questions. Differentiation will be by outcome.

Guided writing. Work with **lower attainers** on question 2.

Plenary
1 Ask pupils how their reading lists compare with Peter's. Write any extra ideas on the board.

2 Do pupils find that their opinions change as they read a book, as Beth's did? What might they write about in a reading log?

ICT For activities linked to this lesson see **PAGE 102**

HOMEWORK

Pupils complete **PCM 3**. They could ask someone at home to answer the questions too.

Link to reading objective

- To identify the features of reading diaries.   5.1 T21

Assumed prior knowledge

- Describing own reading habits.   4.3 T10
- Discussing preferences and reasons.   3.3 T9

Planning suggestion

This unit can be used as the basis for work on **recording ideas and reflections**, including diary writing and making notes about things of interest such as films, plays or sports events.

LESSON TWO

WRITING

- Explain the lesson objective: *to write your own reading log.*

- Pupils will need to choose what they are going to write about. Ask for some suggestions. Remind them that it can be any kind of text.

- Write some ideas on the board, e.g. *an information book they have just started; a CD Rom they have been using; something in a newspaper which surprised or worried them.*

- Refer to Peter's and Beth's logs which you read yesterday. Remind them that they can use notes and lists to sort out their ideas.

- Model the process by starting to write your own log. Emphasise that it is more personal than a review.

- Before they start their own logs, remind pupils of these questions:

   – How do you **feel** about the text? e.g. characters, events or ideas

   – What are your **ideas** and **opinions**?

   – What things **puzzle** you?

   – What would you like to **find out next**?

   Remind pupils to date each entry, because it is interesting to look back at your log later, and see how your ideas and feelings change.

Group activities: differentiation

All pupils write reading logs, working individually, and preferably in near silence. **Lower attainers** can use **PCM 4** for support.

Guided writing. Write your own reading log alongside the group.

Plenary

Invite pupils to read extracts from their logs. Offer to read your own. Point out examples of note form, questions, changing feelings, etc. Did the activity help pupils to sort out their ideas?

EXTENDED WRITING

Pupils continue writing their log.

YOU WILL NEED

- **OHT 3** – Reading Log
- **PCM 4** – Reading Log

ICT For activities linked to this lesson see **PAGE 102**

WATCH OUT FOR ⚠

▸ Difficulty distinguishing between log and book review.
▸ Lack of personal engagement.

3

The Dark Streets of Kimball's Green • FICTION

MAIN WRITING OBJECTIVE

• **To write in the manner of the writer, using paragraphs to organise.**

5.1 T15

Word and sentence level objectives

• To use adverbs to qualify verbs in writing dialogue. 5.1 W10

LESSON ONE

YOU WILL NEED

• **Pupil's Book** pages 9–10
• **OHT 4** – Kimball's Green
• **PCM 5** – Character chart
• **PCM 6** – Homework

MODEL TEXT

• Explain the lesson objective: *to identify features of style and how the author gives life and character to the people in her story*.

• Read the extract aloud. Individual pupils read the dialogue in parts.

• Look at the first five paragraphs in detail. Discuss how the paragraphs focus on different things, e.g. dialogue, action, description. Ask pupils:

– Who is speaking in the first paragraph?

– Who is the second paragraph about?

– What are your first impressions of Mrs Vaughan? *she is mean, does not like Emmeline*

– What details give you that impression? *Mrs Vaughan's angry language; her roughness in combing Emmeline's hair*

– How do you think Joan Aiken wants us to feel about Emmeline? *sorry for her*

– How does the author make you feel this way? *'dashed anxiously', 'flinching face'*

Word and sentence level work

1 Ask pupils to pick out the adverbs used for each character: *Mrs Vaughan – furiously, sharply; Emmeline – anxiously*
What do they tell us about the characters?

2 How might Mrs Vaughan speak if she was a sympathetic character?

Group activities: differentiation

All pupils complete questions 1 and 2. **Lower attainers** can use **PCM 5** for support with question 1. **Higher attainers** can go on to complete question 3.

Guided reading. Find evidence for character traits.

ICT For activities linked to this lesson see **PAGE 102**

Plenary

1 Ask pupils how they think Emmeline feels about Mrs Vaughan.

2 Share ideas about how Mrs Vaughan would treat Emmeline when they were alone.

HOMEWORK

Using **PCM 6** pupils start compilling a word bank of adjectives and adverbs to describe Mrs Vaughan and Emmeline.

Link to reading objective	
● To investigate how characters are presented.	5.1 T3

Assumed prior knowledge	
● Character sketches.	4.1 T11
● Paragraphing.	4.1 T15
● Dialogue rules.	3.3 S4
● Adverbs.	4.1 S4

Planning suggestion

Character studies could be a theme for the week. You could look at the different ways in which characters are presented through description and dialogue. This unit can be linked to Unit 5.

LESSON TWO

YOU WILL NEED

● **OHT 5** – Writing frame
● **PCM 7** – Writing frame

WRITING

● Recap the work done so far.

● Explain the lesson objective: *to write the next part of the story.*

● Tell pupils that in the next part of the story the Welfare Lady leaves and Mrs Vaughan shuts Emmeline out while she goes to bingo.

● From their homework notes, ask pupils to suggest adjectives and adverbs for Mrs Vaughan and Emmeline. Use them to describe how the characters speak and behave.

● Draft the first paragraph together.
 – What does Mrs Vaughan say and do?
 – How does she speak?
 – What does she do then?

● Draft the second paragraph. Ask pupils:
 – What does Emmeline say and do?
 – How does Emmeline feel?

● Read the paragraphs through. Revise where necessary.

Group activities: Differentiation

All pupils complete the question. **Lower attainers** can use **PCM 7**.

Guided writing. Work with **lower attainers** to shape paragraph 3.

For activities linked to this lesson see **PAGE 102**

Plenary

Ask pupils to select one part they are really pleased with and one part that needs improving in their writing.

EXTENDED WRITING

Ask pupils to write about what happens next. What happens when Mrs Vaughan comes back?

WATCH OUT FOR

▸ Lack of identification with Emmeline's feelings.
▸ Incorrect paragraphing in dialogue (higher attaining pupils).

4

Concrete Poems ● WORD PLAY

MAIN WRITING OBJECTIVE

- **To convey feelings or moods in a poem through the careful choice of words and phrases.**   5.1 T16

Word and sentence level objective

- To revise and extend work on verbs, focusing on tenses.   5.1 S8

LESSON ONE

YOU WILL NEED
- **Pupil's Book** pages 12–13
- **OHT 6** – The Witch's Cat

MODEL TEXT

- Explain the lesson objective: *to read different types of concrete poetry and think about personal preference.*

- Explain that in concrete poetry the layout of the words reflects and helps to create meaning.

- Read 'The Witch's Cat'. How are the words arranged? *in the shape of a cat, with words for the whiskers and ears, and the last word in the shape of a cat's tail*

- Read 'Snake' aloud, emphasising the absence of punctuation. Ask pupils why they think 'Snake' has no punctuation. *It gives the impression of continuous movement.*

- Identify differences between 'The Witch's Cat' and 'Snake'. *'The Witch's Cat' describes what the cat looks like. It is like a story written in the shape of a cat. It is in the past tense, punctuated. 'Snake' describes the snake moving, in the present tense with no punctuation.*

Word and sentence level work

1 Look at the verbs in 'The Witch's Cat'. Underline them.
  – Are they all in the same tense?
  – Which verbs are not written in the past tense? *stare and glare*
  – Why do you think the poet did this? *to emphasise the cat's eyes, make the impression of them more immediate*

2 Change all the verbs to the present tense. Discuss how this affects meaning. *It is more immediate, the cat is more threatening.*

Group activities: differentiation

In pairs, **all pupils** answer both questions, expressing personal preferences and referring to the texts.

Guided reading. Support **lower attainers** by looking at just one poem for question 2.

Plenary

Ask pupils to explain the reasons for their choice of favourite poem. Focus on responses to 'Quiet Secret'.

ICT For activities linked to this lesson see **PAGE 102**

HOMEWORK
'Quiet Secret' is written in the shape of a pond. Ask pupils to think of a place they would like to write a poem about.
They should make a list of descriptive words and phrases to use in the poem.

Link to reading objectives

- To analyse and compare poetic style, use of form; to justify personal tastes.
  5.1 T7
- To investigate word play, relating form to meaning.
  5.1 T8

Assumed prior knowledge

- Expressive and descriptive language.
  4.2 T4

Planning suggestion

You can use this unit to introduce **word play** and conveying **meaning** and **mood**. You could produce a class display of concrete poems.

LESSON TWO

WRITING

- Explain the lesson objective: *to write concrete poems.*

- You are going to write a concrete poem together quickly. Then you are going to start another, more complicated one.

- Choose something simple, such as a plant. With the pupils, select the words you will use: *petal, stem, leaf, roots.*

- Ask pupils how the way you write might be different if the plant were a) a thistle or b) a daffodil. *You might write the words in a jagged spiky way for a thistle; in a jolly, bobbing way for a daffodil.*

- Decide what sort of plant you are writing about. Use the words to build up a picture on a blank OHT. It may help to start with a feint outline of the shape.

- Explain that you are now going to work on a poem in the shape of a snail.

- Brainstorm 'poetic' words and phrases you could use. Remind pupils that they are trying to convey meaning and mood. What verb tense will be most appropriate?

OHT 7
- Begin to write some of the words and phrases in the shape of the snail. Show how words can be arranged in a spiral to form the shell.

Group activities: differentiation

PCM 8
In pairs, pupils choose either to write a snail poem using **PCM 8** or a concrete poem on any subject they choose. They can use their homework notes to help them. Differentiation will be by outcome.

Guided writing. Work on using precise details and description.

Plenary

Look at two snail poems. Ask pupils to respond constructively.

EXTENDED WRITING

Pupils finish their concrete poems and write them out neatly for display or for inclusion in a class book.

YOU WILL NEED

- Blank OHT
- **OHT 7** – Outline of snail
- Flipchart
- **PCM 8** – Outline of snail
- Selection of poetry books which include shape poems

For activities linked to this lesson see **PAGE 102**

WATCH OUT FOR
▶ Long phrases and sentences.
▶ Pure description.
▶ Lack of detail.

5 The Angel of Nitshill Road

● CHARACTER

MAIN WRITING OBJECTIVE

- **To write new scenes or characters into a story.** 5.1 T15

Word and sentence level objectives

- To use adverbs to qualify verbs in writing dialogue. 5.1 W10
- To understand how dialogue is set out. 5.1 S7

LESSON ONE

YOU WILL NEED

- **Pupil's Book** pages 15–16
- **OHT 8** – Extract
- **PCM 9** – Character web

MODEL TEXT

- Remind pupils about the different ways of making characters in stories seem real – by describing:
  – what they look like; what they do; what they say (dialogue).

- Explain the lesson objective: *to look at how dialogue makes characters come alive.*

- What a character says and how they say it, tell the reader a great deal about them. It may make the reader like or dislike them, or feel sorry for them. The words need to sound exactly right for their character.

- Anne Fine is very good at realistic dialogue. The dialogue in this extract makes it clear who is the villain and who is the victim.

- Read the extract aloud. What are pupils' first impressions of the characters?

- Look at lines 11–41 in detail. Ask pupils:
  – What words or phrases tell you that Barry is the villain? *"He's weird"*; *poked mark in the chest; spiteful and horrid*
  – What words and phrases show that Mark is the victim? *stumbled, last as usual, tripped over his own feet, thick bottle glasses*

Word and sentence level work

1 Ask pupils to pick out the verbs and adverbs which describe how Barry speaks: *jeered, snorted, scornfully, taunted.*
What do they tell us about his character?
2 Do the same for Celeste.

Group activity: differentiation

All pupils complete questions 1 and 2. **Higher attainers** can move on to complete question 3 using **PCM 9**.

Guided reading. Support **lower attainers** with questions 1 and 2.

ICT For activities linked to this lesson see **PAGE 102**

Plenary

Ask some pupils to show the class their character webs for Barry. Ask pupils to contribute words, phrases and short sentences to describe Celeste and/or Mark. Draw a character web on the board using the words they suggest.

HOMEWORK

Explain that in the next lesson you will be writing two new characters into the story. Ask pupils to make a list of character traits for a villain and a victim.

46

Link to reading objective

● To investigate how characters are presented. 5.1 T3

Assumed prior knowledge

● Character descriptions. 4.1 T11
● Speech marks. 3.3 S4
● Powerful verbs. 4.1 S3
● Adverbs. 4.1 S4

Planning suggestion

This unit can be used as part of a week looking at how **characters** are presented through description and dialogue. This unit can be linked to Unit 3 and to Unit 29.

LESSON TWO

WRITING

● Explain the lesson objective: *to write two new characters in to the story.*

OHT 9

● Make two character webs, one for a villain and one for a victim, using pupils' homework ideas.

● Ask pupils to contribute names for the two characters, and some character traits. Suggest they add some original ingredients, e.g. *female villain.*

● As a class, decide on a situation in which the characters meet. Imagine they are arguing. Decide together what has happened to make them argue. Ask pupils to think about how they might speak to each other. (Although the focus is on dialogue, you could include a brief description of what the characters are doing.)

● When you have enough ideas draft the first few lines of dialogue together. Use verbs and adverbs to describe how the characters speak.

● Remind pupils of the rules for setting out dialogue.

● Comment as you write, rejecting pupils' ideas if they do not sound right for that character. Use slang, incomplete sentences, and interruptions.

Group activities: differentiation

All pupils complete question 1. **Higher attainers** can move on to complete question 2, adding a third character to the dialogue.

Guided writing. Work on speech idioms.

Plenary

Read from work in progress. Is the dialogue convincing? Suggest some improvements.

EXTENDED WRITING

Develop these characters further by writing the opening to a story about them. This could then be extended over time. The ending could be written as further work for **Unit 29 Hunt the Baby.**

YOU WILL NEED

● **OHT 9** – Character web for villain and victim

 ICT For activities linked to this lesson see **PAGE 102**

 WATCH OUT FOR
▶ Insecure knowledge of dialogue rules.
▶ Difficulty in sustaining character.

6

Working Children • PLAYSCRIPT

MAIN WRITING OBJECTIVES

- To write own playscript, applying conventions learned from reading; include production notes.   5.1 T18
- To annotate a playscript, in preparation for performance.   5.1 T19

Word and sentence level objective

- To explain the difference between synonyms.   5.1 W7

LESSON ONE

MODEL TEXT

- Explain the lesson objective: *to revise the features of a playscript, and annotate to show how you would read it.*

- Explain the setting for this scene. Read the first two lines, as spoken by Harry and Beth. Choose two confident readers to continue in these two parts, while you read the rest.

- Go back through the first part of the script marking words and phrases as you talk about them. Add directions for how the lines should be spoken.

  – How are Beth and Harry feeling? *miserable, hungry, helpless*

  – How should their lines be read? *pleadingly, sadly, etc.*

  – What impression do you get of the two ladies? *cross, mean, disgusted*

  – How should their lines be read? *meanly, haughtily*

  – What extra information could you give? *stage directions – important when planning a performance*

Word and sentence level work

Explain synonyms. Synonyms are words that have the same, or similar meanings. Ask pupils to look at the text to find a synonym for hungry (starving) and horrible (disgusting, filthy).

Group activities: differentiation

All pupils prepare the extract on **PCM 10** for a group performance. Encourage them to think about actions (stage directions), how the characters will speak and any other information that will help bring the play to life. **Higher attainers** can move on to annotate the rest of the scene on **PCM 11**.

Guided reading. Practise reading the scene aloud emphasising **how** characters speak.

Plenary

Ask a group of pupils who have completed **PCM 11** to perform the second half of the scene – taking account of stage directions. Other pupils to listen and respond constructively.

YOU WILL NEED

- **Pupil's Book** pages 18–20
- **OHT 10** – Playscript extract
- **PCM 10** – Playscript extract 1
- **PCM 11** – Playscript extract 2

ICT For activities linked to this lesson see **PAGE 103**

HOMEWORK

1 Ask pupils to make a list of adverbs to describe how words are spoken, e.g. *loudly, meekly.*
2 Ask pupils to find two synonyms for each of these adverbs: *sadly, quietly.*

Link to reading objectives

- To understand dramatic conventions.   5.1 T5
- To develop an active attitude towards reading and empathising with characters.   5.1 T9

Assumed prior knowledge

- To prepare, read and perform playscripts.   4.1 T5
- To understand how scenes start, how dialogue is expressed.   4.1 T6
- To write playscripts, using known stories as a basis.   4.1 T13

Planning suggestion

You can use this unit as an introduction to **playwriting and performance.** Pupils' own scenes can be performed and evaluated at the end of the week.

LESSON TWO

WRITING

- Recap the work done yesterday. Refer to the homework. Ask a couple of pupils to write adverbs on the flipchart.

- Explain the lesson objective: *to write the next part of the story in play form.*

- Read the next part of the story aloud (top of the OHT). Then go through it again, marking the text in preparation for rewriting it in play form:

  – underline speech

  – use a different colour for each character

  – put brackets around what might be stage directions.

- With the pupils, refer to the annotated text, and write the first part of the scene in the space provided. For example:

Scene 2

A tumble-down house in a very run-down area of the city.

Harry: (*worried*) Where are we, sir?

Group activities: differentiation

All pupils annotate the text on **PCM 12**. They should then go on to write the scene out in play form. **Lower attainers** can use **PCM 13**.

Guided writing. Work with the **lower attainers**, helping them to look for clues in the text about how characters' lines should be spoken.

Plenary

Ask one group to read the scene aloud. Invite positive responses from other pupils on expression, characterisation and use of actions.

EXTENDED WRITING

Pupils finish writing their playscripts and practise reading aloud together.

YOU WILL NEED

- **OHT 11** – Outline of beginning of Scene 2
- **PCM 12** – Outline of Scene 2
- Flipchart
- **PCM 13** – Playscript Writing Frame

 For activities linked. to this lesson see **PAGE 103**

WATCH OUT FOR

- ▶ Insecure knowledge of conventions of setting out playscript.
- ▶ Difficulty in using stage directions which give clues about characters' thoughts and feelings.

7

People Poems • METAPHOR

MAIN WRITING OBJECTIVES

- To write metaphors and similes.   5.1 T17
- To convey feelings through carefully chosen words and phrases.   5.1 T16

Word and sentence level objective

- To discuss, revise and edit writing.   5.1 S3

LESSON ONE

MODEL TEXT

YOU WILL NEED
- **Pupil's Book** page 22
- **PCM 14** – Homework

- Explain the lesson objective: *to explore metaphors and similes.*

- Recap the term *simile*. Give an example or two.

- Introduce the term *metaphor*. A metaphor makes an idea even more vivid by saying that something actually *is* something else.

- Remind pupils about the special language of poetry which often compares ideas with something you can see or touch or smell.

- The writer Sandy Brownjohn has invented a marvellous way of writing metaphors about people.
  - *You start by thinking of someone you have strong feelings about*
  - *Then you think of a piece of furniture that reminds you of them*
  - *Then an animal, a bird, a time of day, a flower, a food ... and so on.*

  The metaphors can be in any order. Using this idea, Adam wrote 'My Headteacher' when he was eight.

- **PB** Read Adam's poem aloud. Ask pupils:
  - Do you think Adam likes his headteacher?
  - Why do you think that?
  - How do you think his headteacher might be like a magician?
  - Why do you think Adam chose red for the colour of the door?

Word and sentence level work

PB 1 Adam has used adjectives to clarify the picture. Ask pupils:
  - Why do they think Adam chose the word 'bright' for the door?
  - What kind of person might be like a dark or locked door?

2 Ask pupils to suggest some adjectives to describe the headteacher's character: *cheerful, noisy, boisterous, energetic, enthusiastic, fierce*

Group activities: differentiation

All pupils complete both questions. Differentiation will be by outcome.

Guided reading. Focus on describing the features which the metaphor and the subject have in common.

Plenary

Ask pupils to read out their metaphors. Take a vote on whether they fit the character.

HOMEWORK

Pupils complete **PCM 14** identifying similes and metaphors.

Link to reading objective

● To analyse and compare poetic style; to identify shades of meaning.   5.1 T7

Assumed prior knowledge

● Similes.
● Understand the use of figurative language.   4.2 T5
● Experience of revising writing to produce polished poetry.   4.3 T15

Planning suggestion

You can use this unit as the basis for a week of looking at **metaphors**. You could include poems like 'The Sea is a Hungry Dog', by James Reeves, as well as pupils' own work.

LESSON TWO

WRITING

● Explain the lesson objective: *to write a poem using metaphors.*

● Remind pupils of Adam's 'people poem' and re-read it together.

● With the pupils, make a list of the different things in the poem: *furniture, place, animal, bird, flower, sound, time of day, drink, job etc.* If you have time, make up some new categories.

● Choose a sympathetic figure you all know and begin to draft a 'people poem' together. Use pupils' suggestions, adding adjectives and metaphors to create a more vivid picture. Emphasise that it is only a first draft and will need further work.

● Introduce the group activity. Encourage pupils to invent some categories of their own. You may prefer pupils not to write about other members of the class, in case feelings are hurt.

Group activities: differentiation

In pairs, pupils write their own 'people poems'. **Lower attainers** can use **PCM 15** for support.

Guided writing. Focus on editing for economy, and shades of meaning.

Plenary

Read some of the poems. Invite responses. If some poems describe a person everyone knows, ask pupils to guess their identity.

EXTENDED WRITING

1 Pupils revise their poems. and make a neat copy for a class collection.

2 As a class, choose one person for all pupils to write about. Compare metaphors.

YOU WILL NEED
● Blank OHT
● **PCM 15** – Writing frame

 For activities linked to this lesson see **PAGE 103**

WATCH OUT FOR
▶ Bland adjectives.
▶ Superfluous words.

8

Grab the Reader • STORY OPENINGS

MAIN WRITING OBJECTIVE

- **To experiment with alternative ways of opening a story.**   5.1 T11
  (Although this is an NLS reading objective, it is equally applicable
  to children's writing.)

Word and sentence level objectives

- To set out dialogue.   5.1 S7
- To revise verbs – consistency of person.   5.1 S8

LESSON ONE

MODEL TEXT

- Explain the lesson objective: *to look at story openings and identify what makes an effective opening.*

- Ask pupils why they think the opening of a story is so important. *It grabs the reader's attention.*

- The story opening often provides clues about:
  - the type (or genre) of the story, e.g *adventure, mystery, humour*
  - the atmosphere or mood, e.g. *excitement, fear, anger*
  - the characters, e.g. *names, type of person from evidence in text*
  - where and when the story is set, e.g. *place, time, conditions*

- Read the opening of *Vera Pratt and the Bishop's False Teeth*.
  - How does the writer open this story? *using dialogue*
  - Who are the characters? *the bishop and the chauffeur*
  - Where is the story set? *in the grounds of the palace*

- Read aloud the other openings. Discuss how the writer of each opening grabs the reader's interest.

Word and sentence level work

1 Use the first part of *Vera Pratt and the Bishop's False Teeth* to revise the setting out of dialogue.
2 Change the second part of the extract from third to first person. What difference does this make?

Group activities: differentiation

In pairs, pupils complete question 1, using **PCM 16**. **Higher attainers** can move on to question 2.

Guided reading. Work with **lower attainers** to complete **PCM 16**.

Plenary

1 Ask pupils to share their impressions of the main characters.
2 Which opening appeals most and why? Take a vote.

YOU WILL NEED

- **Pupil's Book** pages 24–26
- **OHT 12** Extract from *Vera Pratt and the Bishop's False Teeth*
- **PCM 16** – Openings chart
- **PCM 17** – Homework

ICT For activities linked to this lesson see **PAGE 103**

HOMEWORK

Pupils change the extract on **PCM 17** from the first person into the third person.

Link to reading objective

● To compare story openings and analyse their features.   5.1 T1

Assumed prior knowledge

● Awareness of different aspects of a story e.g. openings.   3.3 T2
● How settings and characters are built up from small details.   4.1 T1
● How settings influence events and characters' behaviour.   4.2 T2

Planning suggestion

You can use **story openings** as a theme for the week. Use pupils' own writing, as well as class library books. You could create a class compilation of story openings.

LESSON TWO

WRITING

● Explain the lesson objective: *to develop two opening paragraphs; one using dialogue, and the other description or action.*

● Agree on two subjects – perhaps a realistic home setting and an adventure or ghost story.

● With pupils, decide which opening strategy to use for each.

● Choose one of the subjects. With pupils, think up several possible opening sentences. Choose the one that works best.

● Brainstorm ideas for the next two or three sentences. Remember to put in some information about characters and setting. Develop this into a short opening paragraph. Remind pupils that they can use 'cliff-hanger' last sentences.

● With pupils, think of an opening sentence for your second subject.

● Read the openings aloud. Check for clarity.

● Remind pupils how important it is to be consistent about 'person'. That is, if you are writing in the third person, do not slip into the first person

YOU WILL NEED

● **PCM 18** – Story opening
● Whiteboard, flipchart or blank OHT

Group activities: differentiation

In pairs, pupils complete question 1. **Lower attainers** can use **PCM 18** for support. **Higher attainers** go on to question 2.

Guided writing. Make sure that the next part of the paragraph links with the opening two sentences. Help pupils to focus on suspense and excitement.

Plenary

Read some opening paragraphs. Evaluate them together. Check that dialogue is set out correctly.

EXTENDED WRITING

Ask pupils to finish planning their story. Make sure they include enough detail. Use the plan as a basis for writing a story.

 For activities linked to this lesson see **PAGE 103**

 **WATCH OUT FOR**
▶ Slipping from third into first person.

53

9

Paper Planes ● INSTRUCTIONS

MAIN WRITING OBJECTIVE

● **To write instructional texts and test them out.** 5.1 T25

Word and sentence level objectives

● To define technical words. 5.2 W9
● To identify imperative form in instructional writing. 5.1 S9
● To revise verb tenses. 5.1 S8

LESSON ONE

YOU WILL NEED

● **Pupil's Book** pages 28–29
● **Prompt Chart 4** – Explanation and Instruction
● **PCM 19** – Evaluation sheet
● A4 paper for making planes

MODEL TEXT

● Brainstorm the important features of instructional texts using the **Prompt Chart**.

● Look at the instructions for making a KH01 Prototype plane.

● Explain the lesson objective: *to evaluate how clear and effective these instructions are.*

● Look at the layout of the page. Ask pupils:

  – Where do you start reading and what do you notice first?

  – What is the purpose of the main illustration? *to show the finished model*

  – Does it do this well? *the illustration is not very realistic*

  – How do the numbers help? *they direct you to each step in order*

  – Would bullet points make the instructions clearer? *not necessarily as text is very short*

  – What are the different ways of making the diagrams clear? *arrows, labels, simple drawings*

Word and sentence level work

1 Discuss and define the technical terms – prototype, A4, guidelines, score, stall, dive.

2 Teach/revise the use of the imperative and present tense in instructional writing (e.g. fold…, press…) Ask pupils to identify examples.

Group activities: differentiation

Pupils follow the instructions to make their own KH01 prototype, then complete the evaluation sheet on **PCM 19**. **Higher attainers** should also list things that could be better.

Guided reading. Work with **lower attainers** to evaluate the instructions.

Plenary

Ask two pupils to launch their planes. Did the planes stall, dive or glide? Were instructions on launching the plane included?

Discuss pupils' evaluations of the instructions and any difficulties they had. Do all their planes look the same and if not, why not?

Ask pupils what improvements could be made to the instructions.

HOMEWORK

Ask pupils to write brief instructions for launching their plane. They should include a labelled diagram.

Link to reading objective

● To evaluate instructional texts for clarity and usefulness.	5.1 T22

Assumed prior knowledge

● Writing instructions.	3.2 T16
● Features of instructional texts.	4.1 T22

Planning suggestion

You can use this unit as the basis for further work on reading, evaluating and writing **instructions**. This could include other models, computer programs or recipes.

LESSON TWO

WRITING

● Ask a couple of pupils to read out the launching instructions for their planes. If possible, display an enlarged copy of their work and evaluate for clarity and effectiveness.

● Explain the lesson objective: *to write instructions for younger pupils to make a paper hat/boat/dart/fortune teller.*

● Explain that together you are going to write instructions for making a paper hat/boat/dart/fortune teller, incorporating the improvements pupils suggested to the instructions in Lesson One.

● Produce the example model you have made. Unfold it and describe the steps you took to make it, noting the number of steps involved.

● Model the process of writing the instructions for the first two steps.

  – Begin with a 'You will need' list.

  – Move on to model the first two steps. Explain that each box will contain a diagram of each step, with the instructions written underneath.

  – With pupils, draft a simple set of instructions with diagrams. Remind them to use the imperative and the present tense.

YOU WILL NEED

● Paper model that you have already made (hat, boat, dart, fortune teller)
● A4 paper
● **OHT 13** – Instruction Writing Frame
● **PCM 20** – Instruction Writing Frame

Group activities: differentiation

In pairs, pupils write instructions and sketch rough diagrams. **Lower attainers** may complete just two steps of the instructions, using **PCM 20** for support

Guided writing. Help pupils to write more succinctly.

ICT For activities linked to this lesson see **PAGE 103**

Plenary

Ask a pair of pupils to present their work. Evaluate it as a group.

EXTENDED WRITING

Ask pupils to revise their instructions and make a neat copy, then try out the instructions on younger pupils. They should evaluate the work using a further copy of **PCM 19**.

WATCH OUT FOR

▶ Difficulty in writing succinctly.
▶ Muddled sequencing.
▶ Unclear diagrams.

10

An Interview with Michael Morpurgo ● PERSONAL EXPERIENCE

MAIN WRITING OBJECTIVES

● **Recording ideas and reflections.**   5.1 T13
● **Making notes and building on them**.   5.1 T26

Word and sentence level objective

● Understanding the difference between direct and reported speech.   5.1 S5

LESSON ONE

YOU WILL NEED

● **Pupil's Book** pages 31–32
● **PCM 21** – Story ideas
● **PCM 22** – Homework

MODEL TEXT

● Explain the lesson objective: *to consider how writers use their personal experience.*

● Introduce the extract from an interview with Michael Morpurgo, who explains how he gets his ideas for writing from his own life.

● Michael Morpurgo lives in Devon. He used to be a primary school teacher. He began by writing with his pupils in the classroom, and trying out his stories on them. He has written over forty stories, many of them involving animals. *The Butterfly Lion* is one of his most popular stories.

● Read the extract aloud. Ask pupils:

– Where do you get your story ideas from? *television, films, own experience*

– What kind of planning do you find most useful?

(Emphasise that there is no one right way – what matters is what works for them.)

– What do you find difficult? You may like to share what you find difficult.

Word and sentence level work

The interview has been taken from a tape-recording. It uses Michael Morpurgo's actual words. With pupils, change the answers to the first two questions into indirect speech. Remind pupils that indirect speech *reports* what someone said and doesn't need speech marks.

Group activities: differentiation

All pupils answer question 1. **Lower attainers** can use **PCM 21** for support. **Higher attainers** can make notes on question 2 for later use.

Guided reading. Work with **Lower attainers** to discuss question 2.

Plenary

Discuss pupils' differing responses to question 1. Start making a list of pupils' ideas for how to get started with a story.

For activities linked to this lesson see **PAGE 103**

HOMEWORK

Ask pupils to think about sharing their writing. Ask them to use **PCM 22**.

Link to reading objective

● Considering how texts can begin with personal experience.   5.1 T4

Assumed prior knowledge

● Familiarity with Morpurgo's work.
● Making notes.   4.2 T21

Planning suggestion

This unit can be used to explore where **story ideas** come from. It links to Unit 11 which looks at story development.

LESSON TWO

WRITING

● Recap some of the main messages from the interview with Michael Morpurgo.

● Explain the lesson objective: *to make notes for a story, starting from pupils' personal experiences.*

● Brainstorm the bare bones of a story set in school. Start with a real event, e.g. a school play, a lost gerbil. Now, using their imagination, pupils turn it into fiction. Something strange happens or disaster strikes. These are their first ideas. Jot down very brief notes.

● Make notes on the setting. Try to capture details in a few telling words and phrases.

● Discuss possible characters and a few *traits*. Pupils can base them on real people but exaggerate their characteristics until they turn into fiction. (Do not use real names, and avoid using members of the class.) Ask pupils:

– What sort of things have you heard people say?

– How do the characters fit into the story?

Group activities: differentiation

All pupils answer all three questions. **Lower attainers** can use **PCM 23** and the notes made in Shared Writing for support.

Guided writing. Work with one group, questioning for further detail.

Plenary

Share a few story ideas. Discuss how pupils could improve their stories.

EXTENDED WRITING

Ask pupils to use their notes to write the first draft of their story.

YOU WILL NEED

● **OHT 14** – Story notes
● **PCM 23** – Story notes

OHT
14

PCM
23

ICT   For activities linked to this lesson see **PAGE 103**

WATCH OUT FOR

▶ Lack of clarity about what the reader needs to know.
▶ Inadequate detail.

11

Michael Morpurgo – Looking at a Manuscript ● PROOF-READING AND EDITING

MAIN WRITING OBJECTIVE

● **To discuss and edit their own writing.**   5.1 S3
(Although this is a sentence objective, it is equally applicable to children's writing.)

Word and sentence level objectives

● To understand the need for punctuation as an aid to the reader.   5.1 S6
● To revise and extend work on verbs.   5.1 S8

LESSON ONE

MODEL TEXT

● Recap how Michael Morpurgo got his ideas for *The Butterfly Lion*.

● Explain the lesson objective: *to look at editing and revising writing.*

Pupils will be looking at the first draft of the opening of *The Butterfly Lion* and noticing the changes the author made.

PB

● Help pupils to decipher the original manuscript by reading the transcript. What do they notice about the author's first draft? *very rough ideas, lots of variations/options in brackets etc.*

● Read the final published version of the story. Ask pupils why they think the author made so many changes to the very beginning of the story. *trying to make it clearer, more gripping, explaining the title*

● Discuss the last sentence of the opening paragraph. Ask pupils what effect the addition of 'I promised them I wouldn't' has on the story opening. *makes you want to find out more, promised who?*

Word and sentence level work

Continue discussing the revision details in the first paragraph, e.g.

– *'they'* and a comma added before *'die'* – to improve the rhythm/impact

– *'To see them, you have to be in the right place'* – makes a clearer link to the butterfly lion.

– *'blue and shimmering'* – more powerful than *'by accident'*.

– *'A long time ago. But I don't forget. I mustn't forget. I promised them I wouldn't.'* – short sentences convey urgency.

Group activities: differentiation

All pupils complete question 1 using **PCM 24**. **Higher attainers** can move on to complete question 2.

Guided reading. Work with **lower attainers** to discuss question 1.

Plenary

Summarise the main reasons for revising – *improving clarity, adding vivid detail, getting the rhythm right.*

YOU WILL NEED

● **Pupil's Book** pages 34–35
● **OHT 15** – Transcript and published version
● **PCM 24** – Transcript and published version

ICT For activities linked to this lesson see **PAGE 104**

HOMEWORK

Ask pupils to carry on with the story started when you were working on Unit 10. Remind pupils to leave space for revising as they write.

Link to reading objective	
● To consider how texts can be rooted in the writer's experience.	5.1 T4

Assumed prior knowledge

● Unit 10 – An Interview with Michael Morpurgo

Planning suggestion

This unit can be used as a follow up to Unit 10, as part of a week looking at story writing.

LESSON TWO

WRITING

- Recap the main reasons for revising work.

- Remind them about Michael Morpurgo's wife. She helps him by being a good response partner. First she picks out bits that work really well. Then she spots the bits that do not sound real, or are too flowery, or are not clear.

- Explain the lesson objective: *to edit and revise your own writing.*

- Show the OHT you have made from the volunteer pupil's work. Ask pupils to point out things that they think work well.

- Where do they think they could improve clarity, detail and rhythm?

- Annotate the OHT, using arrows, omission marks, etc. in different colours to indicate revisions.

- Write out the revised paragraphs on a flipchart or blank OHT.

Group activities: differentiation

In pairs, pupils read each other's drafts of the extended story started in Unit 10, and discuss possible revisions before revising their own work.

Lower attainers without a piece of work of their own can continue to revise the piece of work used in shared writing.

Guided writing. Work on modelling rules for how pupils should respond to their partners' work: *positive and constructive criticism.*

Plenary

Read some examples of work in progress. Comment on improvements in clarity, detail and rhythm.

EXTENDED WRITING

Pupils write the final draft of their story. After writing two paragraphs, they re-read and then revise for clarity, detail and rhythm. They then write another two paragraphs.

YOU WILL NEED

- **OHT** made from a pupil's work, enlarged
- Photocopies of same for those without any writing of their own to revise

 ICT For activities linked to this lesson see **PAGE 104**

 WATCH OUT FOR
▶ Lack of clarity about what the reader needs to know.
▶ Inadequate detail.

MAIN WRITING OBJECTIVES

● **To make notes and to build on them in their own writing.**	5.1 T26
● **To use simple abbreviations in notetaking.**	5.1 T27

Word and sentence level objective

● To investigate which words are essential to meaning.	5.1 S1

LESSON ONE

YOU WILL NEED
- **Pupil's Book** pages 37–38
- **OHT 16** – Spider diagram
- **PCM 25** – School in the 1930s

MODEL TEXT

- Explain the lesson objective: *to see how notes can be made and built upon.*

- Explain that, as part of a topic Rashid and Loretta wanted to compare the lives of children in the 1930s, with their own lives now. First they brainstormed their ideas, then they drew up a spider diagram to show what they would research.

- Explain that a 'spider' diagram is one way of making notes. It helps to organise your ideas. Ask pupils to identify the two main areas of study: *school, leisure*. Circle these on the OHT.

- Next, using a different colour, mark the sub-sections under each heading *age, games etc*.

- Explain that Rashid and Loretta then made notes under each of the headings. Point out abbreviations in their notes such as *sch* and *chn*, and discuss how this speeds up the process of notemaking.

- Discuss the purpose of notemaking. *helps to summarise and organise information; to gain main ideas of text.*

Word and sentence level work

1 Look at the note in the 'School now' column: *leave at 16/some 18*. Ask pupils to expand this into a sentence.

2 Look at the first two sentences of Rashid and Loretta's finished text. Identify the words/phrases which are **not** included in the notes.

3 Ask pupils why they think you need to include these words when you write up notes. *They link the facts into sentences and help other people understand the notes.*

Group activities: differentiation

In pairs, all pupils complete all questions, using **PCM 25** for question 2.

Guided reading. Help pupils to convert notes into sentences by adding details.

Plenary

Evaluate, with pupils, how well they have converted the notes.

Write pupils' ideas for interview questions on the board. Explain that these will be used in the next lesson.

ICT For activities linked to this lesson see **PAGE 104**

HOMEWORK

Ask pupils to brainstorm all the things they might mention if interviewed about their leisure interests and hobbies. They could use a spider diagram to group similar things together, e.g. holidays, hobbies, sports, other.

Ask them to make notes under each heading, using abbreviations.

Link to reading objective

● To discuss the purpose and nature of notes.   5.1 T23

Assumed prior knowledge

● Purpose of notemaking.   3.3 T17
● Identification of key words or phrases.   3.1 T20
● Simple formats to capture key points (flow-charts, diagrams).   4.3 W15

Planning suggestion

You can use this unit as the basis for a week's work on **taking notes** from written and oral sources. Pupils can then write the notes up in the form of a report. The work can be topic related.

LESSON TWO

WRITING

● Explain the lesson objective: *to make notes and use them to write a report.*

● Remind pupils of earlier work on abbreviations.

● Ask the first of the interview questions, prepared in the previous plenary session. Take the responses of two or three pupils, and write these on the board in note form, e.g. *swms, roller bdng, plys CDs.*

● With pupils' help, demonstrate how the notes can be turned into complete sentences, as part of a non-chronological report.

Group activities: differentiation

All pupils ask questions and make notes about each other's leisure interests. After ten minutes, tell pupils to stop their notemaking and move on to classification and drafting.

Guided writing. Review the notes made by **lower attainers** and support them in drafting a report.

Plenary

Ask pupils to comment on the interview and notemaking activity. Look at a few examples of pupils' abbreviated notes. Suggest how these might be expanded into sentences, using the present tense.

EXTENDED WRITING

Pupils edit and rework their drafts into a short report on Children's Leisure Interests and Hobbies.

YOU WILL NEED

● Interview questions from Lesson One plenary

ICT For activities linked to this lesson see **PAGE 104**

WATCH OUT FOR
▶ In notes: writing full words/sentences.
▶ In draft report: not referring to the notes they made; slipping out of the present tense.

MAIN WRITING OBJECTIVES

- **To review and edit writing to produce a final form.**   5.2 T13
- **To revise and develop proof-reading and editing skills**.   5.1 S3

(Although this is a sentence objective, it is equally applicable to pupils' writing skills.)

Word and sentence level objectives

- To understand how words vary across dialects.   5.3 W9
- To investigate clauses.   5.3 S6

LESSON ONE

MODEL TEXT

- Explain the lesson objective: *to look at a story from a different culture and think about it in relation to your own life.*

- James Berry was born and brought up in Jamaica. He writes poetry and short stories based on his own childhood and traditional tales.

- **[PB]** Read the extract aloud. Ask pupils:

  – How do you know this story is from another culture? *dialogue, names, banana truck*

  – What do you think Boy-Don is feeling in the first paragraph? Find the evidence in the text. *excited, tense – 'ears cocked sharp', expectant – 'he listened'*

Word and sentence level work

[PB] 1 Find examples of Jamaican dialect/idioms: *Granny-May love me best, me is the one, bad-talk, lots of things what correct, all obvious.* Change the phrases into standard English.

2 Ask pupils to identify the main clause in the first sentence. *Boy-Don brushed his dog.*

   What is the effect of putting it at the end of the sentence? *builds up suspense*

Group activities: differentiation

[PCM 26] **All pupils** complete questions 1 and 2. **Lower attainers** can use **PCM 26** for support with question 2. **Higher attainers** complete question 3.

Guided reading. Work with **lower attainers** to discuss similarities and differences between Boy-Don's life and their own.

Plenary

Ask pupils to feed back on the similarities and differences between Boy-Don's family life and their own.

YOU WILL NEED

- **Pupil's Book** pages 40–41
- **PCM 26** – Similarities and differences

[ICT] For activities linked to this lesson see **PAGE 104**

HOMEWORK

'Family Life'. Ask pupils to write the first draft of a scene between two members of a family, including some of the typical things they say to each other. Encourage them to use slang/colloquial speech. They should base the scene on their own experiences, but it does not have to be strictly true. (Explain the term 'artistic licence'!)

Remind pupils to use double spacing so that they can revise and edit their work easily in the next session.

Link to reading objective

- To investigate texts from different cultures, considering patterns of relationships in relation to pupils' own experience.   5.3 T1

Assumed prior knowledge

- Character and dialogue.   5.1 T3
- Stories from other cultures.   4.3 T2
- Reading journals.   5.1 T13

Planning suggestion

You can use this unit as a basis for looking at **texts from a range of cultures,** e.g. *Grandpa Chatterji* by Jamila Gavin.

LESSON TWO

WRITING

- Explain the lesson objective: *to use proof-reading marks to revise the first draft of 'Family Life'.*

- James Berry used small clues which told us quickly **when** and **where** the scene was set, **who** the characters were, **why** they were there and **what** they felt about each other. Emphasise to pupils that they should try to do the same.

- Introduce the chart of proof-reading marks and display it.

- Using **OHT 17**, a paragraph on family life, find two good points and two things to improve.

- Revise the draft together, using as many of the proof-reading marks as possible. Concentrate on establishing where, who, why, what. Point out main clauses; add subordinate clauses where necessary to provide more detail. Delete unnecessary repetition. Make the dialogue more colloquial if necessary.

- Correct any punctuation or spelling errors. Make sure everyone understands how to use the marks.

Group activities: differentiation

All pupils complete all questions.

Guided writing. Support **lower attainers**. If necessary they can continue to revise the text they looked at in shared writing, using **PCM 28**.

Plenary

Ask two pupils to read their revised drafts. Evaluate for detail, colloquial speech, and who, what, when, where, why. Discuss how pupils used/altered their own experience.

EXTENDED WRITING

Ask pupils to continue to revise and edit, using proof-reading marks. They should make a clean copy of the finished piece.

YOU WILL NEED

- **OHT 17** – Family life
- **PCM 27** – Proof-reading chart, also large copy for wall
- **PCM 28** – Family life

For activities linked to this lesson see **PAGE 104**

WATCH OUT FOR

- ▶ Limited use of complex sentences.
- ▶ Failure to establish context for dialogue.

MAIN WRITING OBJECTIVE

● **To write own versions of legends.** 5.2 T11

Word and sentence level objectives

● To construct sentences in different ways. 5.2 S8
● To adapt writing for different audiences. 5.2 S3

LESSON ONE

YOU WILL NEED
● **Pupil's Book** pages 43–44
● **Prompt Chart 2** – Myths and Legends
● **PCM 29** – Story Structure

MODEL TEXT

● Explain the lesson objective: *to identify the features of legends.*

● Introduce the extract. It is a legend about a dragon that has been told by people in Poland for hundreds of years.

● Read the extract.

● Using **Prompt Chart 2**, ask pupils to identify any typical features of legends that appear in the story. *real place, perhaps real people; some parts exaggerated; fire-breathing dragon; wise man/hero*

● What parts of the story might have been true, and what parts exaggerated? *Krakus probably existed; the dragon might be an exaggeration of a human tyrant*

● Look at the structure of the story. It begins by introducing the **setting** and **characters**, then establishes the **problem/conflict** (*dragon threatening the village*), then the **hero** (*Krakus*) comes along, there is a **climax** (*the dragon finding his belly full of fire*), a **resolution** of the problem (*the death of the dragon*), and a **happy ending**.

● Explain that most legends follow this pattern.

Word and sentence level work

1 Look at the story language. Point out the order of the words in the first sentence. Discuss the difference that this 'heroic language' makes to the story. Ask pupils to find other examples: *Poor though the people were ... "Of you wisdom, tell us ..." By a trick it shall be overcome.*

2 Highlight examples of powerful verbs and adjectives: *trembled mightiest, slay, undaunted, devoured, blast*

Group activities: Differentiation

All pupils complete question 1, using **PCM 29**. **Higher attainers** should complete questions 2 and 3.

Guided reading. Work with **lower attainers** to identify powerful verbs and adjectives

Plenary

Ask pupils to read out powerful verbs and adjectives which describe Krakus and the dragon.

 ICT
For activities linked to this lesson see **PAGE 104**

HOMEWORK

Pupils should use their story outline to draw a comic strip sequence of *Krakus and the Dragon.*

Link to reading objective

● To identify the features of legends.   5.2 T1

Assumed prior knowledge

● Typical story themes.   3.2 T2
● Verbs; powerful verbs.   4.1 S2/3
● Adjectives.   4.2 S1
● Settings, events, character.   4.2 T2

Planning suggestion

Use this unit to begin a week of exploring **legends from different cultures** (e.g. *George and the Dragon, Cyclops, Gog and Magog*). Look at the typical features and characters of legends. You could link this unit to Unit 17 – Myths.

LESSON TWO

WRITING

YOU WILL NEED

● **OHT 18** – Heroes and Monsters chart
● **PCM 30** – Heroes and Monsters chart

● Explain the lesson objective: *to invent heroes and monsters for your own legends.*

● Remind pupils of the structure of a legend – *setting/character, problem/conflict, hero, climax, resolution, happy ending.*

OHT 18 ● Fill in the Heroes and Monsters chart for Krakus and the dragon. Use some of the verbs and adjectives pupils found yesterday.

● Ask pupils to suggest a modern superhero/ine or monster – e.g. *Spiderman, Batgirl, Godzilla, Dracula.*

● Fill in the chart with pupils' descriptions. Encourage them to use powerful verbs and adjectives.

Group activities: Differentiation

PCM 30 **All pupils** invent their own hero/heroine and monster using **PCM 30**. **Higher attainers** can go on to question 2.

Guided writing. Work with **higher attainers** on question 2, helping them to structure their sentences using heroic language.

 ICT For activities linked to this lesson see **PAGE 104**

Plenary

Ask some pupils to read out their paragraphs describing the monster. Look at the use of heroic language. Which words are particularly powerful? Are the monsters easy to visualise? What improvements could be made?

EXTENDED WRITING

Pupils can use the storyboard (**PCM 29**) to plan the rest of their legend and write the opening paragraph.

 WATCH OUT FOR
▶ Not using heroic language.
▶ Telling the story without exaggeration.

15

The Raggle Taggle Gypsies ●
BALLADS

MAIN WRITING OBJECTIVE

● **To write extensions of poems; substituting own words and ideas.**

5.2 T12

Word and sentence level objectives

● To investigate figures of speech from everyday life.   5.2 W12
● To construct sentences in different ways.   5.2 S8

LESSON ONE

MODEL TEXT

● Explain the lesson objective: *to read and identify the features of a ballad.*

● Explain to pupils that ballads are poems that tell a story, often a sad one. They have been passed on orally, so they have to be easy to remember. They are usually rhythmical and sung to music.

PB

● Read 'The Raggle Taggle Gypsies'. Individual pupils could take parts. Make sure they understand that it is the lord who is speaking in verses 4 and 7.

● Using the **Prompt Chart**, ask pupils to identify some of the typical features of a ballad.

● Discuss the story in more detail.
   – What happens in this ballad? *An unhappy rich lady runs away with the gypsies and her husband can't make her come back.*
   – How many scenes does it have? *scene 1, lady in castle; scene 2, husband rides off to find her; scene 3, gypsies' camp*
   – What impression do you get of the two characters from what they say? *husband only cares about money; lady is wild and reckless*

Word and sentence level work

OHT 19

1 Look at the first three verses in more detail. Ask pupils to look for rhyming words. Point out internal rhymes. Practise clapping the rhythm.

2 Underline examples of poetic language. Ask pupils to rearrange it as ordinary speech, cutting out imagery, e.g. *'Her tears began to flow quickly', 'she went out in the wind with bare feet'.*

What effect do these changes have?

Group activities: differentiation

PCM 31

All pupils work in pairs. The most confident reader should read the ballad aloud before pupils start work on the storyboard (**PCM 31**).

Guided reading. Work with **lower attainers** to decode difficult words.

Plenary

Read through the ballad again. Pupils hold up storyboards for each scene as you read it.

YOU WILL NEED
● **Pupil's Book** pages 46–47
● **OHT 19** – Raggle Taggle Gypsies
● **PCM 31** – Storyboard
● **PCM 32** – Homework: The Ballad of Old Lucy
● **Prompt Chart 3** – Ballads

ICT For activities linked to this lesson see **PAGE 105**

HOMEWORK
Read 'The Ballad of Old Lucy' by Sarah, age 10, on **PCM 32**. Explain that this is a first draft. Ask pupils to answer the questions on the PCM about identifying rhymes and scenes.

Link to reading objectives

● To read a range of narrative poems.	5.2 T4
● To identify typical features of ballads.	5.2 T6

Assumed prior knowledge

● Simple storyboards.	3.2 T7
● Proof-reading and editing.	5.1 S3
● Poems based on structure of other poems.	4.2 T11
● Expressive language/similes.	4.2 T13

Planning suggestion

You can use this unit as the basis for a week looking at **ballads** or at different poetic forms, e.g. sonnet, rap, elegy, narrative poem.

LESSON TWO

WRITING

PCM 32

● Read through 'The Ballad of Old Lucy' together.

● Ask pupils to identify the rhyme scheme, the different scenes, and any other typical ballad features.

● Explain the lesson objective: *to revise and improve the first draft.*

● Ask pupils to pick out a few words or phrases they like, weak lines where the rhythm or rhyme does not work, and words or phrases they think could be improved. Make a note of these.

OHT 20

● Ask pupils to suggest improvements to go in the gaps in the first 3 verses. Choose the alternative that works best. Remember to emphasise rhyme, rhythm, repetition.

● Work together to revise the first verse, demonstrating how to use proof-reading marks. (See **PCM 27**.)

Group activities: differentiation

Pupils continue revising 'The Ballad of Old Lucy'.

PCM 33

Lower attainers can use **PCM 33** for support. If some pupils need a more limited task, they can just work on one verse.

Pupils then move on to question 2, reading the ballad aloud, paying attention to the rhythm and mood.

Guided writing. Concentrate on maintaining a regular rhythm.

Plenary

Ask pupils to read the revised versions aloud, and briefly discuss any improvements that could still be made.

EXTENDED WRITING

1 Pupils finish and polish their revisions.

2 Pupils write a new ballad of their own.

YOU WILL NEED

● **PCM 32** – The Ballad of Old Lucy
● **OHT 20** – The Ballad of Old Lucy (3 verses with gaps)
● **PCM 27** – Proof-reading marks
● **PCM 33** – The Ballad of Old Lucy (with gaps)

 ICT
For activities linked to this lesson see **PAGE 105**

WATCH OUT FOR
▶ Difficulty in maintaining ballad rhythm.
▶ Inaccurate rhymes.

16

An Odd Kettle of Fish

● FIGURES OF SPEECH

MAIN WRITING OBJECTIVE

● **To write extensions of poems using the same structure.** 5.2 T12

Word and sentence level objective

● To investigate figures of speech from everyday life. 5.2 W12

LESSON ONE

MODEL TEXT

● Explain the lesson objective: *to look at the difference between 'figurative' and 'literal language'.*

● Explain the terms figurative and literal. Many everyday expressions or *idioms* are figurative rather than literal. For example, you do not mean it literally when you say someone is 'taken for a ride' or is 'a pain in the neck'.

● James Thurber is a famous American comic writer and cartoonist. When he was a child, he used to think that everyday figures of speech were meant literally. Read aloud the extract on page 49.

● Ask pupils to identify some of the idioms, or figures of speech, and note them down. *skeleton key, under a cloud, up in the air, lost his head*

● Explore the literal meaning of 'under a cloud'. *There's a black cloud over your head.*

● What is the figurative meaning of 'lost his head'? *got confused/ panicked*

● Ask pupils to think of more examples of everyday figures of speech. Add them to the list and leave it on display.

Word and sentence level work

Integrated with text level work above.

Group activities: differentiation

All pupils complete questions 1 and 2. **Lower attainers** can use **PCM 34** for support. **Higher attainers** can move on to question 3.

Guided reading. Go through the literal meaning of more idioms.

Plenary

Share some definitions of Thurber's idioms. Ask for more contributions to the class list of figures of speech.

YOU WILL NEED

● **Pupil's Book** page 49
● **PCM 34** – Figures of speech
● **PCM 35** – Homework: Proverbs

ICT For activities linked to this lesson see **PAGE 105**

HOMEWORK

Pupils explain the meaning of the proverbs on **PCM 35**, and illustrate the literal meaning with a simple drawing. (If necessary, lower ability pupils can complete the exercise from group activities.)

Link to reading objective

- To understand the differences between literal and figurative language. 5.2 T10

Assumed prior knowledge

- Figurative speech, metaphors.
- Similes.
- Everyday wordplay and expressions. 5.1 T8

Planning suggestion

This unit can be used as part of a week looking at different forms of poetry and exploring figures of speech.

LESSON TWO

YOU WILL NEED

- **Pupil's Book** pages 50–51
- **OHT 21** – First three verses of 'An Odd Kettle of Fish'
- **PCM 36** – Writing frame

WRITING

- Recap Lesson One and ask pupils to explain the difference between figurative and literal language.

- Explain the lesson objective: *to read a humorous poem that uses figurative language and write more verses of your own.*

 ● Read aloud the poem 'An Odd Kettle of Fish'.

- Ask pupils how this poem fits in with what they were working on yesterday? *everyday figurative expressions taken literally*

- Look at the pictures and ask pupils what these add to the poem. *they show the literal meaning, add humour*

 ● Annotate the first three verses of the poem. Ask pupils to identify the pattern of each verse. *first line – who said or did something; second line: the idiom; third line in brackets – taking it literally*

- With pupils, choose one of the idioms collected in Lesson One and follow the pattern to write an additional verse. Draw a picture of the literal meaning.

Group activities: differentiation

All pupils write and illustrate another verse. **Lower attainers** can use **PCM 36**. **Higher attainers** can write more than one verse.

Guided writing. Support pupils in following the verse pattern.

Plenary

Read out some of the new verses and display the drawings. Look particularly at the literal meanings. Comment on the humour.

EXTENDED WRITING

Pupils revise and edit their verses (they may like to write a few more) and produce in a final form with illustrations for inclusion in a class anthology.

WATCH OUT FOR
▶ Confusion in reproducing the verse pattern.
▶ Lack of understanding of figurative and literal meanings.

17

Lord Krishna's Flute ● MYTHS

MAIN WRITING OBJECTIVE

● **To write their own version of myths.**   5.2 T1

Word and sentence level objectives

● To construct sentences in different ways.   5.2 S8
● To punctuate complex sentences.   5.2 S5

LESSON ONE

YOU WILL NEED
● **Pupil's Book** pages 53–54
● **Prompt Chart 2** – Myths and Legends
● **PCM 37** – Story notes
● **PCM 38** – Homework

MODEL TEXT

● Explain that, in every time, place and culture, people have told stories which have been passed on from generation to generation. Many of these myths are about gods and goddesses and often explain why things are as they are. For example, why the sun sets every evening; why there is winter every year.

● Explain the lesson objective: *to explore the structure of myths*.

PB
● Read *Lord Krishna's Flute* asking two pupils to read the parts spoken by the boy and Lord Krishna. Explain that this is a myth from India.

● Using the **Prompt Chart**, discuss the features that make this story a typical myth. *god comes to earth and takes on human form; use of magic; explains something in nature*

● Look at the setting and mood. What effect do the descriptions have on the story?

Word and sentence level work

PB
1 Look at the opening sentence. What clues are there that this is the beginning of a myth? *'A long, long time ago'; god comes to earth and becomes human*

2 Look at the final sentence. What clues are there that this is the ending of a myth? *'To this day...' explains something in nature today*

3 Look at the way the writer uses long sentences to add detail to the story. For example, the opening sentence of the last paragraph could read: *'The boy turned into a bird. He began to sing the song of Krishna's flute.'* However, the author tells us exactly how it happened and gives us a description of the bird.

4 Ask pupils to find other examples of complex, descriptive sentences.

Group activities: Differentiation

All pupils complete question 1. **Lower attainers** can use **PCM 37** for support. **Higher attainers** can go on to question 2.

Guided reading. Work with **lower attainers** to discuss question 2.

Plenary

Ask two pupils to re-tell the story in their own words.

HOMEWORK

Pupils complete **PCM 38** looking at the differences between myths and legends. Read the headings and instructions to help them.

Link to reading objectives	
● To identify the features of myths.	5.2 T1
● To understand the effects of imagery.	5.2 T10

Assumed prior knowledge	
● To map out texts showing development and structure.	5.1 T14
● Stories from other cultures.	4.3 T1

Pupil's Book pages ● 53–54

Planning suggestion

Make **myths** a theme for the week. If possible explore a range of myths from around the world.

LESSON TWO

WRITING

- Recap the work done so far on myths.

- Explain the lesson objective: *to write the missing middle part of a myth.*

- Read the beginning and ending of 'How the Magpies Raised the Sky'.

- Ask pupils how they think the magpies might have 'raised the sky'. Brainstorm ideas and record them on a flipchart. Remind them that the gods and some magical happening could be involved.

  (In the actual myth, the birds prop up the sky with sticks. The sun rises and breaks through the darkness and there is joyous birdsong.)

- With pupils, select one idea and develop it into a sequence of events. Take the first event and describe it in a paragraph. Model the use of longer sentences, punctuation and description.

- Read it through with pupils, checking for clarity.

Group activities: Differentiation

Pupils work in pairs to plan the 'middle' part of the story. They will need **PCM 39** to help them.

Guided writing. Support **lower attainers** in planning a sequence of events.

Plenary

Ask 2 or 3 pupils to explain their ideas for the middle of the story. Ask the rest of the class to evaluate and make suggestions for improvement.

EXTENDED WRITING

Pupils continue writing, 'How the Magpies Raised the Sky'.

YOU WILL NEED

- **OHT 22** – 'How the Magpies Raised the Sky'
- Flipchart
- **PCM 39** – 'How the Magpies Raised the Sky'

 For activities linked to this lesson see **PAGE 105**

WATCH OUT FOR

▶ Variation in the use of language: ie not maintaining traditional story mode.
▶ Inaccuracies in punctuation and setting out speech

MAIN WRITING OBJECTIVE

● **To use and acknowledge sources in their own writing.** 5.2 T23

Word and sentence level objective

● To collect and spell technical words from other subjects. 5.2 W9

LESSON ONE

MODEL TEXT

- Explain the lesson objective: *to look at how sources are acknowledged when writing a report based on information texts.*

- Tell pupils that you are going to look at a report, paying particular attention to where the writer got the information from, and how sources of information are acknowledged.

- Discuss why it is important to let readers know which sources were used to gather information. *so that people can find out about the subject; so they can check your facts*

- Explain that the details are usually given in a 'bibliography'.

- Read the opening paragraph of the report.

- Ask pupils if they know anything about blue whales and make a list on the board under the heading *'before reading'*.

- Read the rest of the report and ask pupils to identify the key facts.

- Discuss how the footnotes help you to understand the text. *they give you more information, explain technical terms*

- Look at the bibliography. Ask pupils what they notice about the organisation. *alphabetically ordered by author surname, title, publisher, date of publication*

Word and sentence level work

1 Discuss why inverted commas are used around 'giant comb', in paragraph 4. *quotation from one of the sources, e.g. somebody else's words*

2 Which specialist words are used? e.g. *migrate, baleen, krill, blowholes*

3 Which words can be understood by reading the text? Which require the help of a dictionary or encyclopaedia?

Group activities: differentiation

All pupils complete questions 1 and 2. **Lower attainers** can use **PCM 40** for support. **Higher attainers** move on to question 3.

Plenary

Ask pupils to tell you what they have learned about the blue whale from reading the report, and make another list under the heading *'after reading'*.

YOU WILL NEED

- **Pupil's Book** page 56
- **PCM 40** – All your own words
- **PCM 41** – Homework

HOMEWORK

Ask pupils to make notes on **PCM 41** about what they knew before reading the report about the blue whale, what they learned from reading it, and what else they would like to know.

PB

PB

PCM 40

Link to reading objective

- To discuss what is meant by 'in your own words' and when it is appropriate to adapt and quote.   5.2 T20

Assumed prior knowledge

- To make notes for different purposes.   5.1 T26
- Identification of key words and phrases.   4.2 T21
- Use of simple abbreviations in notemaking.   5.1 T27

Planning suggestion

You can use this unit to introduce **research skills** ahead of beginning work on a class topic. Alternatively you can continue to look at the features of non-fiction texts: technical vocabulary, footnotes, glossary, bibliography.

LESSON TWO

WRITING

- Recap on the homework and make another list under the heading 'what I would like to find out'. Explain that this is a good way to develop research skills.

- Explain the lesson objective: *to research a class topic, make notes and write a bibliography of the sources used.*

OHT 23

- Model the process of planning areas of research, and recording information. First include the name of the class topic, e.g. *The Ancient Egyptians*.

- With pupils, decide which main aspects will be researched, e.g. clothes, buildings, beliefs, etc. Write these under the heading *What I want to find out*. Choose one of these to focus on.

- Give pupils a small selection of books, and ask them to scan the pages to gain key facts. Give them two or three minutes to do this before asking them to feedback to you.

- Write the information in note form under the heading *What I learned*.

- If appropriate, use a direct quotation, within inverted commas, and note the source: *author's surname, title, publisher, date and page number.*

- Remind pupils of the need to acknowledge sources of information. Show them how to record author, title, publisher and date.

Group activities: differentiation

PCM 42

All pupils complete all questions. **Lower attainers** use **PCM 42**. Display the **Prompt Chart** to help all pupils.
Guided writing. Work with **lower attainers** to write a bibliography.

EXTENDED WRITING

Ask pupils to use their notes to prepare a first draft of a report about their area of research.

YOU WILL NEED

- Selection of non-fiction books, CD ROMs or other sources linked to a current topic (different levels of difficulty)
- **OHT 23** – Researching information
- **PCM 42** – Researching information
- **Prompt Chart 5** – Factual Report

ICT For activities linked to this lesson see **PAGE 105**

WATCH OUT FOR !
- ▶ Direct copying of text, without quotation marks and references.
- ▶ Use of technical words without explanation.

19

From Ice to Water • EXPLANATION

MAIN WRITING OBJECTIVES

- **To convert notes into text.** 5.2 T21
- **To plan, compose and edit a short explanatory text.** 5.2 T22

Word and sentence level objective

- To ensure that, in using pronouns, it is clear to what or to whom they refer. 5.2 S10

LESSON ONE

MODEL TEXT

- Introduce the lesson objective: *to read and note the features of explanatory texts.*

 PB

- Look at the 'Melting ice' chart. Explain that Hayley recorded her predictions, observations and explanations on a chart. These notes were later used as the basis for a piece of writing.

- Ask pupils to summarise what was done, what she thought would happen, and what actually happened.

- Look at the final column. Ask pupils why the last column is important. *It explains why the cubes melted in the way they did.*

OHT 24

- Read Hayley's explanation of her experiment. Ask pupils:

  – What is the purpose of this piece of writing? *It describes and explains the results of Hayley's experiment.*

  – Which features of an explanatory text can you find? Use the **Prompt Chart** as a reference. *introductory statement, impersonal language, what happened and why, causal connectives, present tense*

Word and sentence level work

OHT 24

1 Make a note of the causal connectives in the text: *because, cause.* Ask pupils to identify other connectives.

2 Find the pronouns used in the text, and the noun to which they refer.

Group activities: differentiation

All pupils complete both questions.

Guided reading. Work with **lower attainers**, helping them to explain what each paragraph is about.

Plenary

Ask some pupils to read out their explanations, and invite comments.

YOU WILL NEED

- **Pupil's Book** pages 58–59
- **Prompt Chart 4** – Explanation and Instruction
- **OHT 24** – Hayley's explanation

HOMEWORK

Ask pupils to think of a topic they know quite a lot about and makes notes for a short explanation of it. Offer suggestions to those who need guidance, e.g.:
Why leaves fall from trees in autumn.
What causes thunder.
You could link it to an experiment done in science. Encourage pupils to think of paragraph headings when planning what to include.

Link to reading objective

- To read a range of explanatory texts, investigating features such as causal and logical connections: *when, after, because, etc.*   5.2 T15

Assumed prior knowledge

- Brief notes into connected prose.   4.2 T22
- To write explanations of a process.   4.2 T25

Planning suggestion

You can use this unit as the basis for looking at **explanations**. Look at the features of written explanations, including using notes as a basis for writing them. You could link this unit to work in science, explaining the results of an experiment, for example.

LESSON TWO

WRITING

- Ask for a volunteer to give their explanation, using their homework notes. Does the explanation say what happens and why?

- Introduce the lesson objective: *to write a short explanation*.

- Use the volunteer pupil's work (or notes from a class experiment if you wish) to model a short explanation.

- Brainstorm a short introductory paragraph (one or two sentences) which summarises the subject.

- Plan the order of the explanation using paragraph headings.

- Collect and emphasise the use of connectives – time: *next, after that, then*; and causal: *because, as a result of*.

- With pupils, compose the first paragraph. Model the use of pronouns to help the writing flow, making it clear to what they refer.

Group activities: differentiation

Pupils use their homework notes to compose a short explanation. **Lower attainers** can continue the work from the shared writing. All pupils can use **PCM 43** for support if necessary.

Guided writing. Work with **lower attainers**. Check that they give reasons for things happening.

Plenary

Ask one or two pupils to read their work aloud. Using the **Prompt Chart,** ask others to comment on the features of the explanation.

EXTENDED WRITING

1 Pupils finish their explanation. Ask them to make sure that each paragraph links with the one before.

2 Ask pupils to make their own annotated diagram.

YOU WILL NEED

- **OHT 25** – Explanation Writing Frame
- **PCM 43** – Explanation Writing Frame
- **Prompt Chart 4** – Explanation and Instruction
- Flipchart

 For activities linked to this lesson see **PAGE 105**

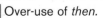 **WATCH OUT FOR**
▶ Over-use of *then*.
▶ Description of *what* happens but not *why*.

20

Mountain Bikes ● EXPLANATION
AND INSTRUCTION

MAIN WRITING OBJECTIVE

● **To write explanatory texts.**   5.2 T22

Word and sentence level objectives

● To write for different purposes.   5.2 S3
● Technical words.   5.2 W9

LESSON ONE

YOU WILL NEED
● **Pupil's Book** pages 61–63

MODEL TEXT

● Explain the lesson objective: *to look at a page from a hobby booklet in detail before planning their own*.

PB ● Ask pupils what they might expect to find in a book on mountain bikes. Then look briefly at the cover and contents page reproduced in their books.

● Discuss the text type: *non-fiction, report, instructions, explanation*. Check that pupils understand the distinctions – a report gives you information about something, instructions tell you how to make it or use it, and an explanation tells you how it works.

● Point out sections of the text as you look through it. Ask pupils:

  – Can you find any instructions?

  – Can you find any explanations?

● Point out that instructions and explanations can be mixed together, e.g. *Pedalling tells you how to do something and explains why*.

● Discuss the page layout. Ask pupils:

  – Why is the first paragraph in bigger print? *It is the main message.*

  – Why are there several separate sub-headings? *to help you find your way around the page, to make things clearer and easier to read*

Word and sentence level work

PB 1 Look at the language of explanation – present tense, third person, arranged in paragraphs, using diagrams.

2 What audience do pupils think this book was written for? Point out how the language and illustration suits the audience: *clear layout, short sentences, colourful action pictures*.

Group activities: differentiation

All pupils complete questions 1 to 3.

Guided reading. Work with **lower attainers** to help them understand the differences between instruction and explanation.

Plenary

Ask pupils to sum up the features of a good information book. Leave the list displayed for the next session.

ICT For activities linked to this lesson see **PAGE 106**

HOMEWORK

All pupils decide on a subject for their own hobby booklet. Encourage them to choose something they enjoy such as football, computer games, collecting things. Ask them to jot down some headings for the information they will include and think about any explanations that will be needed.

Link to reading objectives	
● To investigate features of explanatory texts.	5.2 T15
● To investigate features of instructional texts.	5.1 T22

Assumed prior knowledge	
● Instruction.	4.1 T22
● Using diagrams.	4.2 T20

Planning suggestion

You can use **hobby books** as your theme for the week. You could begin by evaluating library books on hobbies, then move on to the *Mountain Bikes* unit in detail. Complete the week by writing hobby book pages.

LESSON TWO

WRITING

● Explain the lesson objective: *to plan and draft an information booklet about a hobby of their own.*

● Explain that the finished booklets will be short, but the pages will have the same kind of layout as *Mountain Bikes*.

● Ask one or two pupils to describe their homework ideas. Use one of their ideas as a basis for shared writing, or pick a popular hobby such as swimming. Using the eight-page booklet layout, start to sketch out the headings on the appropriate pages.

● Keep the structure simple: Introduction, how to start, what you will need, where to go, some techniques, safety, glossary. Explain that different hobbies will need different headings.

● Choose one page of your booklet and start to plan it out in more detail. Indicate possible sub-headings, illustrations and text.

Group activities: differentiation

In pairs, pupils plan their own hobby booklet. **Lower attainers** can choose to continue the topic from shared writing. They can use **PCMs 44** and **45** for support.

Guided writing. Support pupils in labelling diagrams clearly.

Plenary

Look at work in progress and evaluate it using the list on the board, or the **Prompt Chart**.

EXTENDED WRITING

Pupils revise, edit and proof-read their hobby booklets, taking time and care to produce a polished final version, good enough for the library.

YOU WILL NEED

● **OHT 26** – Booklet layout
● **PCM 44** – Booklet layout
● **OHT 27** – Page layout
● **PCM 45** – Page layout
● **Prompt Chart 4** – Explanation and Instruction

For activities linked to this lesson see **PAGE 106**

WATCH OUT FOR
▶ Muddled instructions.
▶ Unclear diagrams.

Feathered Friends

● NON-CHRONOLOGICAL REPORT/RECOUNT

MAIN WRITING OBJECTIVE

● **To write a short non-chronological report.**   5.2 T22

Word and sentence level objectives

● To define and spell technical words from work in other subjects.   5.2 W9
● To use pronouns clearly.   5.2 S10

LESSON ONE

MODEL TEXT

● Explain the lesson objective: *to compare personal and impersonal styles of writing.*

● Refer to the **Prompt Chart**. Explain that reports give factual information, and should be concise and accurate. They should follow the criteria for impersonal style.

PB ● Tell pupils that the two short pieces have the same subject – pigeons – but are written in different styles. Read each piece from the Pupil's Book.

● Ask pupils:

  – Which writing is mainly personal and based on observation? *Eleanor's*

  – What features make it personal? *personal involvement; personal comment, past tense, describes a particular event.*

  – Which piece of writing is impersonal, and based on research? *Robert's*

  – What features make it impersonal? *present tense; impersonal pronouns; facts; use of technical words; no personal opinion*

Word and sentence level work

PB 1 Ask pupils what the impersonal pronoun 'it' refers to in line 3 (first example) of Eleanor's writing. *the wing*

2 Ask pupils to find examples of technical terms in Robert's report. *rump, abdomen*

Group activities: differentiation

PCM 46 **All pupils** complete all three questions. **Lower attainers** can use **PCM 46** for support with question 3.

Guided reading. Discuss the differences between personal and impersonal writing.

Plenary

Ask selected pupils to explain their responses to questions 1 and 2.

Discuss responses to question 3, and how paragraph headings can help to indicate subject matter.

YOU WILL NEED

● **Pupil's Book** pages 65–66
● **Prompt Chart 6** – Personal/Impersonal style
● **PCM 46** – Robert's text
● **PCM 47** – Homework: Changing style

HOMEWORK

The piece of writing on King Charles Spaniels (**PCM 47**) mixes personal and impersonal styles of writing. Ask pupils to rewrite it as an impersonal report. Remind them that to do this they will have to change some words and cut some sentences.

Link to reading objective

- To read a range of non-chronological reports and explanatory texts, investigating features of impersonal style. 5.2 T15

Assumed prior knowledge

- To make and fill out notes. 4.2 T22
- To collect information and re-present. 4.2 T23
- To note key points. 5.1 T26
- Pronouns. 3.3 S2
- To summarise key ideas. 4.3 T24

Planning suggestion

This unit can be used as part of a week looking at writing **non-chronological reports**. This could be linked to work in other subjects.

LESSON TWO

WRITING

- Quickly go through the homework. Ask pupils to point out which features were not appropriate to impersonal writing. Ask one or two pupils to read out their revised impersonal report.

- Explain the lesson objective: *to plan a short non-chronological report, written in impersonal style.*

- Take a subject that pupils know a lot about, e.g. *spiders, cats, Ancient Egypt.*

- Brainstorm facts and information about the subject/topic. Remind pupils that these will fit into the category of impersonal writing. Write notes on the OHT.

- Using coloured pens, underline related facts, e.g. *habitat, physical features, food, etc.*

- Give each group of related facts a paragraph heading.

Group activities: differentiation

All pupils attempt the writing task in mixed ability groups. Choose pupils who can write quickly and fluently to act as scribes for each group. All groups can use **PCM 48** for support.

Guided writing. Work with each group on the features of an impersonal report. At the editing and revision stage, encourage pupils to look critically at their own writing.

Plenary

Read through the group reports or reports in progress. Ask pupils to evaluate in terms of impersonal writing features.

EXTENDED WRITING

Ask pupils to plan and write a short impersonal report about a person, place or subject they know well (it could be related to a class topic).

YOU WILL NEED

- **OHT 28** – Planning an impersonal report
- **PCM 48** – Report writing frame
- Picture or other stimuli for chosen subject for shared writing (optional)

 ICT For activities linked to this lesson see **PAGE 106**

WATCH OUT FOR
► Inconsistency of agreement between nouns, pronouns and verbs.

Gran Can You Rap?

● PERFORMANCE POETRY

MAIN WRITING OBJECTIVE

- ● **To use performance poems as models to write, and to produce polished poems through revising, redrafting and presentation.** 5.3 T11

Word and sentence level objectives

- ● To use punctuation marks accurately. 5.3 S4
- ● To identify a range of prepositions. 5.3 S3

LESSON ONE

MODEL TEXT

- ● Ask pupils whether they have heard or read rap music or poetry. Originally raps came from the Caribbean. They are generally in dialect or slang. They have a strong beat and a fast pace, like a dance, and they rhyme.

- ● Explain the lesson objective: *to prepare a performance of* 'Gran Can You Rap?'

PB
- ● Read the rap at a lively pace, emphasising the rhythm and rhyme. Encourage pupils to clap to the rhythm once they have picked it up.

- ● Ask pupils:
  - – Which line is repeated in each verse? *I'm the best rapping Gran this world's ever seen.*
  - – How does the chorus vary each time? *The first two 'nonsense' words change – tip-top, slip-slap becomes nip-nap, yip-yap etc.*

- ● Recite the chorus together. Discuss how you could increase the speed and volume for the last verse.

Word and sentence level work

PB
1 Gran raps all over the place! Identify all the prepositions: *past, through, down, round, up.*
Think of more examples: *on the table, in the bath, over Glasgow, under ground, by the playground.*

2 Read the rap aloud once again. Ask some pupils to mark the commas, question marks and full stops with claps, finger clicks and a 'raspberry' respectively. They need to be alert and come in on time so that the beat keeps going!

Group activities: differentiation

All pupils work in **mixed attaining** groups to prepare readings of the rap.

Guided reading. If necessary, put **lower attainers** in one group and provide support.

Plenary

Ask a group of pupils to perform 'Gran Can You Rap?'. Evaluate the performance.

YOU WILL NEED
- ● **Pupil's Book** pages 68–69
- ● **PCM 49** – Homework

ICT For activities linked to this lesson see **PAGE 106**

HOMEWORK

Pupils learn 'Gran Can You Rap?' by heart. They will need to take home a copy of the rap on **PCM 49**.

Link to reading objectives

- To read, rehearse and modify performance poetry. 5.3 T4
- To select poetry and justify choices. 5.3 T5

Assumed prior knowledge

- Poems with repeating phrases. 3.1 T12
- Performance/oral poetry. 3.2 T4
- Patterns and rhyme. 4.2 T7

Planning suggestion

You can use this unit as the basis for introducing a week on **performance poetry**. You could look at classic performance poems such as 'Macavity the Mystery Cat' by T S Eliot or 'Night Mail' by W H Auden.

LESSON TWO

WRITING

YOU WILL NEED

- **OHT 29** – Writing frame
- **PCM 50** – Writing frame

- Explain the lesson objective: *to write raps*.

OHT 29
- Refer back to the original rap as a model. Ask pupils to point out where rhymes are needed (lines 1 and 2; 3 and 4). Work together on writing the verse. Use some of the prepositions suggested in Lesson One.

- Invent new pairs of words for the chorus, e.g. *bip-bop, clip-clap, flip-flop*

Group activities: differentiation

PCM 50
Lower attainers complete question 1, using **PCM 50** for support.
Higher attainers complete question 2.

Guided writing. Work with **higher attainers**, helping them to compose their own rap.

 ICT For activities linked to this lesson see **PAGE 106**

Plenary

Ask pairs of pupils to recite their rap. Evaluate as before.

EXTENDED WRITING

Ask pupils to revise their rap in the light of the plenary discussion. Pupils work on their own and then compare their rap with a partner.

WATCH OUT FOR
▶ Difficulty in maintaining rap rhythm.

MAIN WRITING OBJECTIVE

- **To write from another character's point of view.**   5.3 T7

Word and sentence level objective

- Basic conventions of standard English; agreement between nouns and verbs   5.3 S1

LESSON ONE

YOU WILL NEED

- **Pupil's Book** pages 71–72
- **OHT 30** – Extract
- **PCM 51** – Points of view chart
- **PCM 52** – Homework

MODEL TEXT

- Explain the lesson objective: *to look at the point of view of a story and how it affects the reader.*

- Explain that most stories can be told from different points of view. Ask pupils if they know of any stories written in this way? e.g. *The True Story of The Three Little Pigs* (Wolf's point of view) *by Jon Scieszka.*

- Tell pupils that you will be looking at an extract from *Stig of the Dump,* by Clive King, and that you would like them to imagine the incident from the point of view of the youngest Snarget.

- Read the extract aloud. Invite some fluent readers to join in by reading the dialogue. Ask pupils:

  – Who is telling the story? *a narrator – the author, Clive King*

  – From whose point of view do we see events? *Barney, the main character*

  – How does the youngest Snarget feel in paragraph 2? *excited, enjoying the chase*

  – How does the youngest Snarget feel in paragraph 3? *frightened, shocked, cannot believe his eyes*

  – What did the youngest Snarget think was going to happen when Stig caught him? *that Stig would eat him*

Word and sentence level work

Look at the first two paragraphs in detail. Annotate the OHT.

1 Discuss/revise the agreement between nouns and verbs and the consistency of tenses and subject.

2 Look at the use of both past and present tense. Discuss why conventions are necessary and why they are important.

For activities linked to this lesson see
PAGE 106

Group activities: differentiation

All pupils complete the exercise (using **PCM 51**) in groups which include one fluent reader.

Guided reading. Work with **lower attainers** to explore the extract from a different point of view.

HOMEWORK

Ask pupils to think of slang and dialect words and phrases for the items listed on **PCM 52**. Alternatively, they could complete the notes begun in group activities.

Plenary

How is the youngest Snarget's point of view different from Barney's?

Link to reading objectives	
● Point of view and how it affects the reader.	5.3 T2
● Changing point of view.	5.3 T3

Assumed prior knowledge	
● How to make notes from reading.	5.2 T20
● Purpose of paragraphs.	4.1 T15
● Dialogue in stories.	3.3 S4

Planning suggestion

You can use **narrative viewpoint** as a theme for the week. Look at different examples.

LESSON TWO

WRITING

YOU WILL NEED
● Flipchart or blank OHT

- Explain the lesson objective: *to write the story from a different character's point of view.*

- Ask pupils to feed back their notes on the extract from the youngest Snarget's point of view.

- Jot these down and use them as a basis for modelling an opening paragraph, written from this point of view.

- Explain that the last sentence from the original text would not appear in this rewrite, as it is written from Barney's point of view, and the young Snarget does not know where Barney is or what he is feeling.

- Jot down notes about the content of the following paragraphs, asking pupils for ideas. Remind them to think about how the youngest Snarget feels, as well as what happens.

Group activities: differentiation

All pupils rewrite the extract from the youngest Snarget's point of view. **Higher attainers** answer question 3.

Guided writing. Focus on the description of thoughts and feelings.

Plenary

Ask three pupils to read aloud from their work in progress. Ask other pupils to comment on expression of feelings and viewpoint, and on level of detail.

EXTENDED WRITING

1 Pupils could write a few paragraphs more to tell what might have happened next.

2 Ask pupils to check and revise their work.

 For activities linked to this lesson see **PAGE 106**

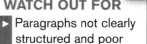 **WATCH OUT FOR**
▶ Paragraphs not clearly structured and poor links between them.
▶ Inconsistent use of first person and past tense.

MAIN WRITING OBJECTIVE

● **To construct, present and evaluate an argument.**   5.3 T19

Word and sentence level objectives

● To adapt writing for different audiences.   5.3 S2
● To use the conventions of standard English.   5.3 S1
● To be aware of the differences between spoken and written English.   5.2 S6

LESSON ONE

MODEL TEXT

● Explain the lesson objective: *to read some pupils' views about transport and to see how persuasive their arguments are.*

● Look at the magazine article 'Alternative Transport'. Explain that the writing is based on interviews. Briefly comment on the layout – the heading; how the picture indicates whose opinion you are reading.

● Read the article aloud. Ask pupils:
  – What is the main disadvantage of solar-powered cars that Lee and Kim think of? *no sun in this country*
  – What does Sarah think is especially good about them? *no fumes*
  – Who do you agree with?
  – Why do Sarah and Lee think it wouldn't work to share cars? *people wouldn't bother, they don't like to share*
  – What do you think?

Word and sentence level work

1 Look at Lee's interview in more detail. Discuss how it would differ if Lee was writing his arguments down, rather than being interviewed. *argument would have more formal structure, less use of colloquial language*

2 Ask pupils what they notice about the style of writing of the interview. *informal, chatty*
Identify examples of this – *abbreviations: 'doesn't', 'isn't'; casual language: 'all the stuff'*

3 Pick out some devices that Lee uses to persuade us: *'the best way', 'buses are better', 'a good idea'.*

Group activities: differentiation

All pupils complete questions 1 and 2, using **PCM 53** for support with question 1. **Higher attainers** can go on to question 3.

Plenary

Look at pupils' lists for and against the different ideas for alternative transport. Which was the favourite idea? Which was the least favourite? What persuaded them for or against the ideas?

YOU WILL NEED

● **Pupil's Book** pages 74–75
● **OHT 31** – Lee's interview
● **PCM 53** – For and Against
● **PCM 54** – Homework

HOMEWORK

Pupils complete **PCM 54** listing arguments for and against being taught at home via the Internet.

Link to reading objectives

- To read and evaluate a range of texts for persuasiveness and clarity.   5.3 T14
- To collect persuasive devices.   5.3 T15

Assumed prior knowledge

- Point of view and persuasive writing.   4.3 T23
- Notemaking.   5.2 T20

Planning suggestion

This unit can be used as part of a week on **persuasive writing and argument**. It links to Unit 26. Try to look at several examples from different kinds of writing.

LESSON TWO

WRITING

- Explain the lesson objective: *to write an argument.*
- Referring to pupils' homework notes, brainstorm some of the advantages and disadvantages of lessons at home via the Internet.
- Using the **Prompt Chart** remind pupils of the criteria for persuasive writing. Decide democratically which argument you're going to promote.
- Make notes under the following headings:

  What we are arguing for

  Arguments for

  Arguments against

  Why arguments against are wrong

  Conclusion

- Now begin to write the argument together using the writing frame.
- If necessary, change the writing frame to suit what you want to say (it is important that pupils know they can do this too).

YOU WILL NEED

- Completed homework from Lesson One
- **OHT 32** – Writing Frame
- **PCM 55** – Writing Frame
- **Prompt Chart 7** – Persuasive Writing

Group activities: differentiation

Pupils work in pairs to complete the writing frame begun in the shared session or write alternative arguments of their own. **Lower attainers** can use **PCM 55** for support.

Guided writing. Help pupils to alter the writing frame to suit their own needs.

Plenary

Ask a pair of pupils to read out their argument. Who was persuaded in favour of the argument? Take a vote.

EXTENDED WRITING

Rewrite your notes as a letter to the editor of a newspaper. If possible send it to your local newspaper. Remember to use standard English in a formal letter.

WATCH OUT FOR

- Difficulty in keeping to a logical sequence in argument.
- Failure to identify appropriate key words in notemaking.
- Use of casual language in writing argument.

MAIN WRITING OBJECTIVE

● **To write discursively about a novel.**   5.3 T10

Word and sentence level objectives

● To punctuate complex sentences.   5.3 S4
● To understand how clauses are connected.   5.3 S6

LESSON ONE

MODEL TEXT

YOU WILL NEED
● **Pupil's Book** pages 77–78
● **PCM 56** – Thought bubbles
● **PCM 57** – Point of view chart

● Explain the lesson objective: *to look at point of view and how it affects our response to a novel.*

PB

● Introduce the extract. *The Wreck of the Zanzibar* is told through Laura's diary. Read the extract aloud.

● The story is narrated in the first person. Ask pupils:

– What effect does this have? *it helps you to imagine being there, as if it's really happening; you see things through Laura's eyes*

– What do you think Laura is feeling as she rows out to the wreck? *excited, determined, desperate*

– What clues are there in her writing to suggest this? *active verbs: ran, leapt, pulling hard; use of exclamation marks; repetiton: 'At last, at last, at last!'*

Word and sentence level work

PB

1 Look at the second paragraph of the extract. Ask pupils how the opening sentence might divide into shorter sentences and write the new text on the board. (e.g. So, I took up my father's oar. I took my share of the weight on my shoulder. I left Father behind on the dunes. We ran the gig down the beach and into the sea.)

2 Repeat the exercise with the second and third sentences.

3 Discuss the differences and point out that the text flows much more smoothly in longer sentences, and is much more atmospheric.

Group activities: Differentiation

PCM 56

All pupils complete question 1, using **PCM 56**. **Higher attainers** move on to question 2, using **PCM 57**.

PCM 57

Guided reading. Work with **lower attainers** to discuss what they have read recently.

ICT For activities linked to this lesson see **PAGE 107**

Plenary

Discuss various types of point of view – ie stories where there is more than one point of view, or where the narrator is an animal.

Recap some of the effects of different points of view.

HOMEWORK
Pupils begin/continue working on their points of view chart, adding more titles. Encourage them to browse through book blurbs, as well as thinking of books they have already read.

● To identify the point of view from which a story is told.

5.3 T2

Assumed prior knowledge

● A general familiarity with Morpurgo's novels (see Units 10 and 11).
● Point of view (see Unit 23).
● Book reviews.

3.3 T14

Planning suggestion

This unit can form part of a week looking at **point of view**. Alternatively it can form part of a week working on making writing flow by increasing the use of complex sentences.

LESSON TWO

WRITING

● Using the **Prompt Chart**, remind pupils of the work they have done on point of view, and of how this affects how you feel about a book and its characters.

● Explain the lesson objective: *to write a book report*.

● Using the writing frame, draft a book report on *The Wreck of the Zanzibar*.

● The first paragraph of the report should be the introduction. It summarises the story so far. This paragraph has been written for you.

● The next paragraph should describe the story's point(s) of view.

● The final paragraph should summarise how the book extract made you feel and what effect the point of view had on your feelings.

● As you write together, try to connect the clauses to make longer sentences.

Group activities: Differentiation

All pupils write the first draft of a book report. **Lower attainers** can use **PCM 58** to help them continue/revise the report from shared writing.

Guided writing. Focus on using connectives to link clauses. Help pupils to summarise effectively.

Plenary

Read one or two of the book reports. How could they be improved?

EXTENDED WRITING

Pupils could write a book report that compares two different characters from a novel. They can use **PCM 59** for support.

YOU WILL NEED

● **Prompt Chart 8** – Points of view
● **OHT 33** – Writing frame
● **PCM 58** – Book report writing frame

 For activities linked to this lesson see **PAGE 107**

 WATCH OUT FOR
▶ Difficulties in close reading for textual clues.
▶ Difficulty in structuring a report logically.

Too Little, Too Late • EDITORIAL

MAIN WRITING OBJECTIVES

- **To set out and justify a personal view.**   5.3 T18
- **To construct an argument and evaluate its effectiveness.**   5.3 T19

Word and sentence level objective

- To understand how writing can be adapted for different audiences and purposes.   5.3 S2

LESSON ONE

YOU WILL NEED

- **Pupil's Book** pages 80–81
- **Prompt Chart 7** – Persuasive Writing
- **PCM 60** – Making sense
- **PCM 61** – Editorial writing frame
- Newspapers with examples of editorial pieces

MODEL TEXT

- Explain the lesson objective: *to read and evaluate an article which is meant to persuade people.*

- Review pupils' understanding of how writing seeks to persuade readers: *gives reasons, appeals to emotions, uses questions, may suggest a solution.* Refer to the **Prompt Chart.**

- Focus on the headline of the article. Where might you see a headline like this? *in a newspaper or magazine*

- Explain what an 'editorial' is. If possible, show children the editorial pieces in several newspapers. Point out that these express a particular point of view.

- Read the article aloud.

  – What information do we get from the opening paragraph? *not enough is being done to halt traffic pollution*

  – Which words show how the writer feels? *'too little too late' – writer is not impressed*

  – Which paragraphs give reasons to support the writer's point of view? *2, 3 and 4*

  – What do you notice about the last paragraph? *sums up argument and what the writer wants to see done*

Word and sentence level work

1 Find words or phrases that are used to persuade readers. *'brave new approach', 'really make a difference', 'look at the facts!'*

2 Look at the short punchy openings to paragraphs 1, 2 and 3. Why is this form of writing used? *to grab reader's attention*

ICT For activities linked to this lesson see **PAGE 107**

Group activities: differentiation

All pupils do questions 1 and 2, using **PCM 60**. **Higher attainers** complete question 3, using **PCM 61**.

Guided reading. Work with **higher attainers** to discuss point of view.

Plenary

Recap on the way a persuasive article appeals to the emotions of its readers.

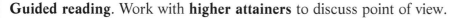

HOMEWORK

Ask pupils to collect other editorials in newspapers, magazines and newsletters. Ask them to think of some issues which are important to them, and which could be used as the subject of a news editorial.

Link to reading objective

- To read and evaluate articles intended to inform, protest, complain, persuade.   5.3 T12

Assumed prior knowledge

- Main features of newspapers.   4.1 T20
- Persuasive writing.   4.3 T18
- Evaluate examples of arguments and discussions, e.g. letters to the press and articles about issues.   4.3 T16

Planning suggestion

You can use this unit as a basis for looking at and developing **persuasive writing**. This unit links with Unit 24.

LESSON TWO

WRITING

- Explain the lesson objective: *to write a news editorial to persuade people of your point of view.*

- Remind pupils that an editorial presents one point of view, and tries to persuade others to this way of thinking.

- Ask pupils to suggest issues which they are concerned about.

- With pupils, select an issue for shared writing (preferably, one on which all or most agree). Allow some time for discussion.

- Plan your argument. Take ideas about what should go under Heading 1.

- Write a couple of sentences to form a short opening paragraph.

- Move on to Heading 2. Brainstorm reasons for holding this point of view. Make notes, putting the most serious point first.

- Finally, make brief notes under Heading 3 and compose an appropriate conclusion.

Group activities: differentiation

All pupils complete question 1. Display the **Prompt Chart** to help them. **Higher attainers** can move on to question 2.

Guided writing. Support the work of **lower attainers**, or those writing a different point of view.

Some pupils may take an opposite point of view from the rest of the class on the issue. If so, help them to prepare their own article. They can use **PCM 62** to help them plan their argument.

Plenary

Read aloud some examples of work finished, or in progress. Identify successful persuasive strategies used.

EXTENDED WRITING

Ask pupils to finish their article, and make a neat copy. They may go on to write another article on an issue of their choice.

YOU WILL NEED

- **Prompt Chart 7** – Persuasive Writing
- **OHT 34** – Planning an article: Writing frame
- **PCM 62** – Planning an article: Writing frame

ICT For activities linked to this lesson see **PAGE 107**

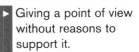

WATCH OUT FOR
- Giving a point of view without reasons to support it.
- Variation in tenses – slipping into past tense.

MAIN WRITING OBJECTIVE

● **To draft letters for real purposes on emotional issues; to edit and present in finished state.**   5.3 T17

Word and sentence level objective

● To write for different audiences and purposes.   5.3 S2

LESSON ONE

YOU WILL NEED

● **Pupil's Book** pages 83–84
● **PCM 63** – Problem page
● **PCM 64** – Homework

MODEL TEXT

● Explain the lesson objective: *looking at problem page letters and their answers.*

● Are pupils familiar with problem pages in magazines?

● These examples come from the Agony Aunt pages in two different magazines. Can pupils explain the term 'Agony Aunt'?

● Choose three confident pupils to read the letters aloud. Read the answers yourself, emphasising their sympathetic but practical tone.

● Ask pupils:

– Who do you think the magazines are for? *children/teenagers*

– What kind of topics do people mainly write about? Are they typical problems for people of your age?

– Which of the agony aunts would you prefer to write to? Why?

● There is a formula for the replies. Ask pupils to identify these three sections in the sample letters: *sympathy; comfort; practical advice.*

Word and sentence level work

1 Ask pupils what tone of voice is used by the Agony Aunts? *understanding, comforting, sympathetic but firm, practical*

2 Pick out words and phrases to illustrate these traits: *'It hurts to lose a mate', 'Time to let go', 'Talk to your teacher', 'it's understandable',*

3 The letters sound like someone talking. Ask pupils to find some examples of colloquial style: *contractions – I'm, he's, it's, don't; idiomatic phrases – 'getting me down', 'drive me mad', 'a brilliant mate', 'brainier than me'*

Group activities: differentiation

All pupils complete questions 1–3, using **PCM 63** for question 1.
Higher attainers complete question 4.

Guided reading. Help **lower attainers** question 2.

ICT For activities linked to this lesson see **PAGE 107**

Plenary

Discuss pupils' opinions. Recap the qualities of Agony Aunts and make a list to display on the wall. Include the formula for replies.

HOMEWORK

Pupils read the problems on **PCM 64** then write notes on what they might reply.

Link to reading objective

● To read and evaluate letters from magazines.   5.3 T12

Assumed prior knowledge

● Letter writing.   3.3 T20

Planning suggestion

Use this unit as part of a week looking at a range of **letters for different purposes**. You could link it to Unit 28 (protest letters).

Note
Some very serious issues may come up during this work.
Be prepared to handle them sensitively.

LESSON TWO

WRITING

● Remind pupils of the main points from Lesson One.

● Explain the lesson objective: *to plan and draft a reply to a problem.*

● Read the letter aloud. Highlight the two problems – reading aloud and answering questions. Ask pupils to identify the writer's main worry. *making a fool of herself*

● Recap the Agony Aunt formula identified in Lesson One

● Brainstorm ideas for a reply. Make notes on the OHT. Do not write it out in full.

Group activities: differentiation

All pupils complete the task. **Higher attainers** should use their homework notes to write an original Agony Aunt response. **Lower attainers** can use **PCM 65** to continue the reply begun in shared writing.

Guided writing. Make up a not-too-serious problem letter together. Help pupils to identify and use some phrases from the letters: *However hard I try; what can/ should I do? Please help me....* Think of a suitable title and signature.

Plenary

Ask pairs of pupils to read the letters and their replies. Evaluate the replies against the checklist made in Lesson One. Would the replies be helpful?

EXTENDED WRITING

1 Ask pupils to begin to draft a new problem letter. The problem can be real or imaginary. They work on their own, then give it to a partner to respond to, or give it to you if they prefer.
2 Ask pupils to reply to a letter composed during the lesson.

YOU WILL NEED

● Agony Aunt checklist (from previous plenary)
● **OHT 35** – Problem writing frame
● **PCM 65** – Problem writing frame

 For activities linked to this lesson see **PAGE 107**

WATCH OUT FOR
▶ Difficulty in keeping to the formula.
▶ Limited knowledge of letter-writing conventions.

Child Labour • PROTEST LETTERS

MAIN WRITING OBJECTIVE

- **To draft and write protest letters for real purposes.**   5.3 T17

Word and sentence level objective

- To write for different audiences and purposes.   5.3 S2

LESSON ONE

MODEL TEXT

- Explain the lesson objective: *to read about a situation which might persuade someone to write a protest letter.*

- Explain that protest letters are used to communicate objections or strong feelings about something.

- Read the extract 'How is a rug made?'. How would pupils feel if this happened to them?

- Explain the term 'premature arthritis'. Why would the children suffer from this? *small hands made to do detailed work for long hours*

- In what other ways could working for 16 hours a day damage your health? *eyestrain, backache, no exercise, no play*

- Why do pupils think the employers use children to make the rugs? *they can pay children less; children's hands are small enough to weave*

- Read the extract about Iqbal Masih, and the explanation of 'bonded labour'. What are pupils reactions to hearing this story? How does it make them feel?

- Explain that tomorrow they will be writing a protest letter about child labour.

Word and sentence level work

1 Look at 'How is a rug made?'. What parts of the text show that the writer has strong feelings about the subject? *exclamation mark, 'it matters little to the bosses', telling us harsh facts*

2 Why do pupils think the article starts with two questions? *to attract your attention, to get you to feel personally involved*

Group activities: Differentiation

All pupils complete both questions. **Lower attainers** can use **PCM 66** for support with question 1.

Plenary

Ask pupils to contribute three main facts about child labour which they might use in a protest letter. Discuss where they might send the letter – newspaper? TV programme? Radio? Amnesty International? UNICEF? Save the Children Fund?

YOU WILL NEED

- **Pupil's Book** pages 86–87
- **PCM 66** – Iqbal's Story
- **PCM 67** – Homework

HOMEWORK

Pupils complete the exercise on **PCM 67**. You may wish to read the story through for them.

Link to reading objectives

● To compare writing which informs and persuades.   5.3 T13
● To read and evaluate protest letters.   5.3 T12

Assumed prior knowledge

● Letter writing.   3.3 T20
● Fact and opinion.   4.1 T19
● Use of paragraphs to organise information.   4.2 T19

Planning suggestion

You can use this unit as the start of a class debate or discussion. You can explore **protest letters** in depth and encourage them to write such letters for real purposes. This unit links to Unit 27.

LESSON TWO

WRITING

● Recap yesterday's information about child labour. On the flipchart draw up a list of significant facts about child labour and the reasons (opinions) why you think it is wrong. Ask pupils to contribute from their homework notes.

● Explain the lesson objective: *to write a letter protesting about child labour.*

● Using the **Prompt Chart** discuss the features of protest letters. Explain that a good protest letter should have:
  – an opening statement saying what you believe or feel
  – the arguments backed up by facts
  – a summary which repeats the opening statement.

● Point out the need for good presentation so that the person you are writing to will take you seriously.

● With pupils, compose a powerful opening sentence. You could start with a question. Remind them of the 'How is a rug made?' article.

● Follow it with a statement of what you believe and why. Remind pupils that they will need to support their opinions with facts.

Group activities: Differentiation

All pupils plan and draft a protest letter using their homework notes. Lower attainers can use **PCM 68** for support.

Guided writing: Focus on including emotive questions.

Plenary

Read out some of the letters. How could pupils make them more persuasive?

Discuss how you could combine the best bits from several letters into a single letter from the class which everyone could sign.

EXTENDED WRITING

1 Swap letters with another pair. Underline the bits you like best and return it.
2 Make a neat copy of your finished version.

YOU WILL NEED

● **Prompt Chart 9** – Protest Letters
● Flipchart headed: *Facts* and *Opinions*
● **OHT 36** – Protest letter writing frame
● **PCM 67** – Completed homework
● **PCM 68** – Writing frame

For activities linked to this lesson see
PAGE 108

WATCH OUT FOR
▶ Lack of logical argument.
▶ Weak connectives.

MAIN WRITING OBJECTIVE

● **To write in the style of an author.**   5.3 T9

Word and sentence level objectives

● To compile a class dictionary of slang.   5.3 W13
● To secure the conventions of standard English.   5.3 S1
● To investigate clauses and connectives.   5.3 S6 and 7

LESSON ONE

MODEL TEXT

● Jacqueline Wilson is an award-winning author. Her stories are always funny but often the heroines have a tough life. They survive by having a sense of humour.

● Explain the lesson objective: *to look closely at the author's style and how she achieves her effects.*

● Read the extract aloud. Ask pupils:

  – Whose point of view is the story told from? *Elsa's*

  – What kind of person do you think she is? *always joking, looking on the bright side, cares about her family, maybe hides her unhappiness behind the jokes?*

  – How does Jacqueline Wilson make the writing sound as if it's Elsa speaking? *uses slang, tells jokes, talks directly to the reader*

Word and sentence level work

1 Elsa tells the story as if she's speaking. Pick out some words and phrases which give that effect: *incomplete sentences; use of slang etc.*

2 Ask pupils to find some examples of slang: *e.g. posh, crummy, hasn't half, super-duper, fantastic, scarpered.* Look up their meanings in a dictionary of slang. With pupils, turn them into standard English.

3 Look at paragraph 2 of the first extract. Compare single clause sentences with the longer sentence, 'We're so poor...'. Identify the connectives – *and, but, so* – that help to make longer sentences.

Group activities: differentiation

All pupils complete questions 1 and 2 using **PCM 69.**
Lower attainers can use **PCM 70** for support with question 2.
Guided reading. Work with **lower attainers** on question 1.

Plenary

Ask some pupils to read their dialogue. Does it sound convincing? Briefly list of some of the main features of Jacqueline Wilson's style – *chatty, slang, funny, etc.*

YOU WILL NEED

● **Pupil's Book** pages 89–90
● **OHT 37** – Hunt the Baby
● **PCM 69** – Connectives
● **PCM 70** – Writing frame

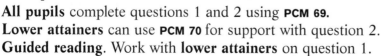

ICT   For activities linked to this lesson see **PAGE 108**

HOMEWORK

Predictions: how will the story end? Pupils either make notes in reading logs in preparation for the next session or finish **PCM 69** on connectives, following guided group work.

Link to reading objective

● To identify point of view and how it affects the reader's response.　　5.3 T2

Assumed prior knowledge

● Point of view. (Unit 23)
● Some acquaintance with stories by Jacqueline Wilson.
● Clauses and connectives.　　4.2 S4
● Rules for writing dialogue.　　3.3 S4

Planning suggestion

Use this unit as part of a week looking at story endings. Try to look at a range of endings by well-known writers.

LESSON TWO

WRITING

● Explain the lesson objective: *to write the ending for* Hunt the Baby *using Jacqueline Wilson's style.*

● Remind pupils of where the extract stopped. Recap some of the significant features: *told in first person, tough characters, realistic dialogue, use of slang, jokes, etc.*

● Display an OHT or enlarged copy of an example of dialogue drafted in Lesson One. Ask pupils:

　– Is the story likely to have a happy ending? *jokes would be out of place for tragedy*

Discuss some favourite story endings and how they tie in with things mentioned earlier.

● Work together on planning about four or five more paragraphs to complete the story, making brief notes. Refer back to the extract for clues.

● With pupils, draft the first sentence of the continuation. Show how to link it with a connective to the end of the previous dialogue: *so/then/suddenly/after a while.*

Group activities: differentiation

All pupils plan and write the ending. **Lower attainers** will probably not have time to revise and discuss their work. Pupils who write particularly slowly could be asked to write two paragraphs only.

Higher attainers move on to question 4.

Guided writing. Work on the use of connectives.

Plenary

Listen to two endings, or several 'favourite parts'. Evaluate against the criteria. Continue the discussion of what makes a good ending.

EXTENDED WRITING

Ask pupils to finish their first draft by revising and editing. Pupils could compare their ending with the original book.

YOU WILL NEED

● **OHT** or enlarged copy of a pupils' work from Lesson One

ICT For activities linked to this lesson see **PAGE 108**

WATCH OUT FOR

▶ Lack of correct dialogue conventions.
▶ Failure to use text clues to imitate style

MAIN WRITING OBJECTIVES

- To write a persuasive leaflet, using numbered lists and bullet points.   5.3 T18
- To construct and evaluate an argument.   5.3 T19

Word and sentence level objectives

- To adapt writing for different purposes and audiences.   5.3 S2
- To revise imperatives.   5.1 S9

LESSON ONE

MODEL TEXT

- Explain the lesson objective: *to look at a persuasive leaflet and evaluate its effectiveness.*

- Use the **Prompt Chart** to revise the criteria for good persuasive writing.

- Introduce the NO SMOKING DAY leaflet.

- Using a sheet of A4 paper, show pupils how the leaflet would be folded so that page 1 is the cover and page 6 is at the back.

- Skim-read the leaflet, helping pupils to use the headings, numbered lists and bullet points to understand the main message.

- Look at the cover in detail. What is catchy about the slogan? *It's a play on words – one expects the phrase to be 'ready steady go'.*

- Discuss pages 2 and 3 and the idea of a countdown to stopping smoking for good. Ask pupils if they think this is effective.

- Look at page 5 of the leaflet – Benefits of stopping for good. Which arguments do they think are the most convincing?

- How does the layout of the leaflet help to get the message across? *clear use of different fonts, bullet points, lists and clear headings*

Word and sentence level work

Revise instructions and the use of the imperative. Look at page 4 of the leaflet, and identify some examples: '*take one day at a time*'; '*save the money*'; '*don't give up*'. Ask pupils to identify others.

Group activities Differentiation

Lower attainers complete questions 1 and 2. They will need **PCM 71** for question 1, and can use **PCM 72** for support with question 2.
Higher attainers complete questions 3 and 4.

Guided reading. Discuss with **lower attainers** how persuasive writing grabs the reader's attention.

Plenary

Recap the four stages in 'Ready Steady Stop!' and summarise their content. Explain that in the next session they will be designing their own leaflet for a No ... Something ... Day. Collect ideas for what this might be, e.g. No Moaning, No Litter, No Quarrelling.

YOU WILL NEED

- **Pupil's Book** pages 92–94
- **Prompt Chart 7** – Persuausive Writing
- **PCM 71** – Benefits of stopping
- **PCM 72** – Poster

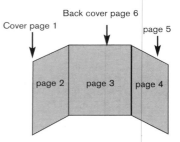

Cover page 1   Back cover page 6   page 5

page 2   page 3   page 4

ICT   For activities linked to this lesson see **PAGE 108**

HOMEWORK

Pupils think of their own ideas for a 'Stop _____ing day', then sketch an idea for a poster and make notes for the text.

PB

PB

PCM 71

PCM 72

Link to reading objective	
● Read and evaluate a range of persuasive texts.	5.3 T14

Assumed prior knowledge	
● Familiarity with leaflets.	
● Persuasive writing.	4.3 T23

Pupil's Book pages ● 92–94

Planning suggestion

Use this unit as the basis for a week looking at a variety of **leaflets**. Pupils should design, draft, edit and evaluate their own work.

LESSON TWO

WRITING

- Explain the lesson objective: *to design a persuasive leaflet.*

- Look at some of their homework ideas. Take a class vote for one idea for a 'No ... Something ... Day', which you will develop into a leaflet.

- Begin writing the leaflet together, starting with the cover. Write the name of the day below the slogan, and a date. Discuss a simple, bold image that you could use on the cover.

- Move on to the next page, Getting Ready. Draft the first stage of the countdown. (The countdown is a simple 3,2,1, but pupils can add more to this later if they wish.) Ask pupils to suggest reasons why they should stop ...., and note them in the space provided.

- Brainstorm ideas for the rest of the countdown and write them on the board. Explain that this will form page 3 of their own leaflet.

- Using the prepared PCM (**PCMs 72** and **73** as a double sided sheet), demonstrate again how the final leaflet will be folded together.

Group activities: Differentiation

Pupils could work in mixed ability pairs. Pupils draft the cover and pages 2/3 of their own leaflet, based on the work from shared writing. They may use the writing frame provided by **PCMs 73** and **74** if needed.

Guided writing. Help pupils to use bullet points and imperatives.

Plenary

Discuss and evaluate some examples of work in progress.

EXTENDED WRITING

Pupils continue working on the leaflet, jotting down ideas for the other sections. Partners could work on a page each.

Make a final version, taking time to lay out the lettering carefully.

YOU WILL NEED

- Notes from yesterday's plenary
- **OHTs 38** and **39** – writing frame
- **PCMs 73** and **74** photocopied as a double sided writing frame.

ICT For activities linked to this lesson see **PAGE 108**

WATCH OUT FOR

► Too much time spent on lettering.
► Text not 'punchy' enough.
► Unclear layout.

OHT 38

OHT 39

PCM 73

PCM 74

Information and Communication Technology

ICT and its place in the UK Curriculum

The curricula for England, Wales, Scotland and Northern Ireland all require that ICT should be used to support writing and learning about language. The Literacy Hour is an ideal starting place for many of these activities. By incorporating ICT activities into the Literacy Hour and other writing sessions, many elements of the ICT Programmes of Study may be taught in 'real' contexts.

The new National Curriculum Orders for England & Wales (published in 1999 for implementation in 2000), the new 5 – 14 Guidelines for Scotland (published in 2000) and the Education Technology Strategy 1996-2000 in Northern Ireland, all give ICT a prominent place across all curriculum areas and give an entitlement for all pupils to achieve ICT capability.

ICT and Literacy

Literacy in the 21st century involves making sense of language and writing in many different contexts. In responding to texts, children must learn to recognise and be critical of the rich range of media; in producing their own writing, they must learn to use different media appropriately to suit their audience and purpose.

Children should be encouraged to explore the extent to which page-layout and design, use of colour, choice of fonts and text styles can enhance their writing. They also have opportunities, through the world wide web and multimedia authoring, to publish for wider audiences and to communicate via e-mail with children throughout the world.

During the Literacy Hour, pupils may be using ICT to support language and literacy development as well as developing their personal ICT capability.

Opportunities to develop the ICT skills associated with these activities can be included in the Literacy Hour and at other times throughout the week. The suggested activities provided in **Models for Writing** offer some starting points.

ICT to support whole class and group work

ICT can support and enhance discursive and interactive whole-class teaching and group work. The range of software available varies from fairly straightforward presentation packages available with standard office-type applications to fully-featured multimedia authoring tools. Interactive whiteboards, wide-format monitors, an LCD tablet with high-powered OHP, daylight projectors or large TV monitors should all be considered as options for presenting to groups. These vary considerably in price and are likely to represent significant capital investments for many primary schools. Teachers should discuss the options available with the ICT Co-ordinator or local advisory service.

When planning to use presentation software, consider what the 'added value' will be to pupils over traditional methods such as big books, flip-charts, blackboard and chalk, video, TV, radio, OHT, whiteboard and marker pen. A major advantage is that your presentation is stored in digital form and may be re-used for other purposes. If your presentation includes input from children during the session, this will also be stored for future use. Furthermore, a multimedia presentation allows a range of media to be used from one single workstation rather than juggling between an OHP, video and big book.

Models for Writing is accompanied by a set of colour OHTs which are an integral part of shared reading and writing. The OHTs contain extracts from model texts, and provide a wide variety of writing and planning frames to support pupils in developing their reading and writing skills. They allow the teacher to model both the reading and the writing processes to the class, and OHT pens can be used to highlight teaching points.

Audio-recording equipment is another valuable ICT tool. For example, when discussing performance poetry it may be used to enable children to experiment with different styles of delivery, evaluating each others' recordings.

ICT for writing, editing and publishing

Using ICT to support children's writing means far more than simply asking them to word-process their text. The use of ICT can help children compose, transform and present text, and will give them a growing understanding and confidence in literacy, language, layout, style and design. Whether the writing and presentation of a text involves illustrating a poem, setting out information in a chart, or annotating a diagram, ICT can be used to support the activity and examples are provided in *Models for Writing*.

When writing, the children can change their work using various tools. Cutting and pasting paragraphs, sentences and words gives children the freedom to experiment with their text and decide the most appropriate way of ordering it. Using the electronic thesaurus allows the children to expand their vocabulary, and the spell-checker gives them the opportunity to check and correct their work. The final piece of writing will have a high standard of presentation that has been developed and adapted to suit the audience and the purpose of the piece.

As far as you are able, it is important to choose appropriate software for these activities. Some word-processing packages are capable of handling text and images to produce more sophisticated work, but if you want the children to begin to learn transferable skills associated with desktop publishing (DTP) you will achieve far better results with a desktop publishing program than with a word-processor.

Teachers who are confident with computers, and who have the appropriate painting or drawing software can also consider the use of ICT to illustrate children's work, where such an activity supports the learning objective.

Writing and the Internet

The Internet provides many opportunities for developing communication skills. Children should think about the emerging styles of writing which are appropriate for e-mail messages and be given opportunities to send and receive e-mail for real purposes. They may have 'net-pals' who will be interested in some of the writing arising from the activities in *Models for Writing*. Some of the activities lend themselves to setting up an e-mail project between schools in the UK using this scheme, or using a unit in the scheme as the starting point for a project with schools in other parts of the world.

Preparing some writing for the school website is another means whereby children will be writing for real and wider unknown audiences. There are two ways in which pupils may 'publish' on the web. They may have produced some writing for print which may be 'showcased' in a gallery on the school website. There may also be opportunities for children to design part of the school website or even their own website.

ICT and *Models for Writing*

On pages 102–108 you will find ICT activities for each unit of *Models for Writing*.

On pages 109–112 you will find a **Glossary of ICT terms**. This explains the ICT terminology used in the activities and gives simple, practical examples of what the terminology means.

Preparation and organisation of activities

In preparing to use ICT with *Models for Writing* teachers should check with the ICT Co-ordinator what hardware and software are available for use with Year 5. It is important to plan the development of ICT resources in consultation with other teachers, the Literacy Co-ordinator and ICT Co-ordinator. Many of the activities and resources prepared for use in one year group may be quickly modified for use by colleagues in other year groups if there is a school-wide policy on how to create and store digital material.

The ICT Co-ordinator will be able to advise on the most appropriate software to use for different applications, in particular when graphics are being created and stored.

Another important co-ordination function is to ensure that children have had the opportunity to learn the basic ICT skills they will need to use in order to carry out some of the activities suggested in *Models for Writing*.

The time taken to prepare the ICT activities for *Models for Writing* will depend on the ICT competence and confidence of teachers, as well as the software and hardware available in school. It may be appropriate for non-teaching assistants to do some of the preparatory tasks under the direction of a Year 5 teacher. Once the basic preparation is done, the resources will be available to, and may be modified and adapted for each class.

It is important to plan how to develop, save and back-up all ICT resources using a systematic and agreed filing structure either on floppy disks or a school network. Discuss the systems with the ICT Co-ordinator and develop a whole-school approach to managing digital resources.

IMPORTANT NOTE:

Several of the following ICT activities instruct you to prepare a text-file of the model text.

It is important to be aware that the keying in and electronic storage of copyright material is a breach of copyright law. The Publisher has obtained permission for the classroom activitites suggested in *Models for Writing*, but the keyed texts should not be stored on a network or otherwise transferred electronically.

If in doubt, consult your Copyright and Licensing Authority document.

Models for Writing: ICT activities

(Please note that these do not include the use of OHTs, which are within the main lesson plans for each unit.)

UNIT	TITLE	LESSON ONE	LESSON TWO
1	Chilham Castle	Prepare a **text file** of the model text. Using a **talking word-processor**, pupils will gain sound-support in evaluating Claire's writing. Using the **text file**, pupils edit it as an informal personal note and send by e-mail to another pupil.	Prepare a **word-bank** including connectives, introductory sentences and words associated with a recent shared experience. This will provide pupils with support for writing and revising a recount or letter to a friend using a **word-processor.**
2	Reading Logs	Using the **Internet**, build up a set of **bookmarks** including sites such as http://amazon.co.uk/ which publish book reviews and interviews with authors. Pupils may submit reviews online for the world to share.	Prepare a simple **database** with an appropriate field structure (title, author, publisher) to include books commonly read by pupils. Use this as a Year group resource to summarise, share and catalogue information about books being read in Year 5.
3	Kimball's Green	Prepare a **word-bank** including adverbs, adjectives, synonyms and key words associated with the model text.	Using the **word-bank** with their **word-processor** provides pupils with support for writing the third paragraph.
4	Concrete Poems	Prepare sample shapes and place text into these to form concrete poems using a drawing or painting package. NB: This activity should not be done using a word-processor.	Pupils explore the use of colour, pattern, fonts, shapes of letters and words in a drawing or painting package to create concrete poems. Discuss how using ICT is different from paper and pencil for creating these effects.
5	The Angel of Nitshill Road	Prepare a **text file** of the model text. Using a **talking word-processor**, pupils will gain sound support to pick out verbs and adverbs. Use the electronic **thesaurus** to select alternatives for the verbs and adverbs.	Prepare a **word-bank** including adverbs, adjectives, synonyms and key words associated with the model text. Pupils write story openings and save them into a **directory** for use in other writing activities.

UNIT	TITLE	LESSON ONE	LESSON TWO
6	Working Children	Prepare a **text file** of the model text, and **word-bank** for stage directions. Using a **talking word-processor**, pupils will gain sound and text support to annotate the script to include stage directions.	Prepare a **template** or **stylesheet** for playscript layout in a **word-processor** or DTP package. Prepare a **text file** of the next part of the play (prose – OHT 11). Pupils use the template and text file to re-write the model text as a playscript.
7	People Poems		Pupils explore the use of shape, fonts, colour and **clip-art** in a drawing or painting package to create illustrations for their poems. They should concentrate on matching their metaphors to the people they describe.
8	Grab the Reader	Prepare a **text file** of the model story openings for revision as a story starter. Use **e-mail** to play 'story chains' either in your own school or with another school using *Models for Writing*. Children add a paragraph to continue the story from another child's opening paragraph.	Prepare story starters based on the final paragraphs of the model text, or use pupils' own story openings. Save these into a **directory** for use in other writing activities.
9	Paper Planes		Prepare a **template** in a **DTP** package with **image boxes** and **text frames**. Pupils use the template to create a set of instructions modelled on the KH01 prototype example.
10	Interview with Michael Morpurgo	Prepare a **text file** of the model text. Pupils use this as the basis for re-writing the copy as indirect speech. They should use the cut, copy and paste functions in the **word-processor**.	Pupils use a **word-processor** to develop their notes into the first draft of a story, saving it regularly. Using 'outline' view in a word-processor or planning software may provide useful support for drafting ideas.

UNIT	TITLE	LESSON ONE	LESSON TWO
11	Michael Morpurgo: Looking at a Manuscript	Prepare sample layouts to illustrate double-spacing, wide margins, **stylesheets** and other layout features which assist in revising manuscripts and discuss the value of these with the class.	Develop the story started in Unit 10 as a shared writing activity using the **word-processor**. Invite an author, playwright or journalist who regularly writes using a word-processor to discuss the advantages of creating copy in digital form. You could try the following **website** which has been set up by the Arts Council and allows you to contact authors: http://www.nawe.co.uk
12	Then and Now	Prepare a table in a **word-processor**. Put in sample text and sentences in the present tense for leisure activities.	The table provides support for pupils in collecting information from questioning their partner, and writing the report using the **word-processor**.
13	Banana-Day Trip	Go to the partner-finding area of the European Schoolnet **website** at http://www.en.eun.org/menu/projects/partners.html and find contacts for an Internet project. **E-mail** links with another school provide children with first-hand examples of both culture and dialect.	Prepare a **text file** of the text to be revised. Pupils make the corrections from proof-readers' marks directly into the **word-processor**.
14	Krakus and the Dragon	Pupils record the powerful, heroic words, using interesting voices and sounds, and explore the use of shape, fonts, colour, clip-art or their own artwork in a drawing or painting package to illustrate them. Incorporate the words, sound and visuals in a presentation using a **multimedia** authoring package.	Using 'outline' view in a **word-processor** or planning software provides useful support for drafting and story-boarding. Save the opening paragraphs into a **directory** for use in other writing activities. Illustrate the stories with **clip-art** or pupils' own artwork and typography in a word-processing or DTP package.

UNIT	TITLE	LESSON ONE	LESSON TWO
15	The Raggle Taggle Gypsies	Prepare a **text file** of the homework text: *The Ballad of Old Lucy* and a **word-bank** with suitable rhyming words. Browse the **Internet** for sites with poetry anthologies and recommend a suitable selection to the children. http://www.bbc.co.uk/education /listenandwrite/home.htm.	Using the prepared text and **word-bank** in a **talking word-processor**, pupils revise the ballad as a collaborative writing exercise. Make audio recordings of a collection of ballads. Illustrate the ballads and, using a **multimedia** authoring package, create an audio-visual anthology.
16	An Odd Kettle of Fish	Prepare a **template** in a **DTP** package with **image boxes** and **text frames** or use a **multimedia** authoring package to create a class anthology of the verses and illustrations produced in this Unit.	
17	Lord Krishna's Flute		Prepare a **text file** of the beginning and ending of 'How the Magpies Raised the Sky'. Using the prepared text and 'outline' view in a **talking word-processor**, pupils develop the middle of the story as a collaborative writing exercise. Use the cut and paste functions to maintain traditional story styles.
18	The Blue Whale		Use an **Internet search engine** and electronic encyclopaedia to find relevant information about the class topic. **Download** and save images and text to share with others. Discuss issues of authenticity and accuracy when using web-based resources
19	From Ice to Water	Using a **word-processor** and selecting a suitable font and and format, write out the notes as an explanation suitable for other pupils. Print the explanation out and see if other pupils can understand it.	In pairs, make brief notes about a simple feature of ICT, for example, 'how a floppy disk works' or 'why it is important to save material regularly'.

UNIT	TITLE	LESSON ONE	LESSON TWO
20	Mountain Bikes	Use a **search engine** on the **Internet** to find Mountain Bike websites. Compare the information available and the styles of presentation with a book or magazine. Discuss the differences and suggest reasons for them.	Prepare a **template** for the booklet in a **DTP** package with **image boxes**, **stylesheets** and **text frames**. Pupils use the template to create their own hobby booklets. They should prepare images in a drawing or painting package and text in a word-processor. This should be a group activity with pupils taking specialist roles such as designer, editor, author, illustrator, proof-reader, researcher etc.
21	Feathered Friends		Prepare a **word-bank** including key words and phrases about the subject selected. Children work in small groups at the computer to write a short report using a **word-processor**. Use the word count feature to check word length and save drafts regularly.
22	Gran can you Rap?	Browse the **Internet** for sites with poetry anthologies and recommend a suitable selection to the children. http://www.bbc.co.uk/education /listenandwrite/home.htm	Make audio recordings of raps and other performance poetry, using a range of sound effects. Illustrate the poems and use a **multimedia** authoring package to create an audio-visual anthology.
23	The Snargets	Prepare a **text file** of the text.	Open two **word-processing** documents and split the window to view both a new, blank document and the prepared text file. Pupils re-write the story from the youngest Snarget's point of view in the blank document by cutting and pasting copy from the original, making changes as appropriate and saving the new file regularly.

UNIT	TITLE	LESSON ONE	LESSON TWO
24	Leave Your Car at Home		Use notes, recorded speech and suitable images to create a presentation outlining the arguments for and against using a **multimedia** authoring package or web-page editor. Present the arguments in a school assembly or upload it to the school website to reach a wider audience.
25	Book Report	Browse some of the **Internet** bookshops such as http://amazon.co.uk/ which publish book reviews and interviews with authors. Pupils may submit reviews online for the world to share.	Review the entries in the **database** created for Unit 2 and add to throughout the year. Analyse the data collected and produce a short presentation about reading in Year 5.
26	Too little, too late	Prepare a **word-bank** including persuasive words and phrases. Children use the **word-bank** and **talking word-processor** to write the first draft of a short, persuasive article for a newspaper. Browse editorials published on the **Internet** at television and newspaper websites. Discuss how these reports differ from printed and broadcast editorials.	Prepare a **template** in a **DTP** package with **image boxes** and **text frames** suitable for the editorial page in a newspaper. Pupils import the copy, lay up the pages and use suitable images to illustrate the editorial.
27	Agony Aunts	Prepare a **word-bank** and collections of phrases typical for use in 'problem page' writing. Children use a **talking word-processor** to write several 'formula' replies to different types of letter. Children use a **talking word-processor** to write sample letters to an Agony Aunt.	Prepare a **template** in a **DTP** package with **image boxes** and **text frames** suitable for Agony Aunt pages in a magazine or newspaper. Pupils import the copy, lay up the pages and use suitable images to illustrate the letters.

UNIT	TITLE	LESSON ONE	LESSON TWO
28	Child Labour		Combine the key points from several letters using a **word-processor** to organise the paragraphs. Visit the Amnesty International website to find out about current campaigns and appeals http://www.amnesty.org/index.html
29	Hunt the Baby	Create a two column table in a **word-processor** for slang words and their definitions. Children start the list using examples from this Unit. Print the first drafts for discussion.	Build the list up as a class activity over two or three weeks, saving it regularly and revising definitions. Sort the list alphabetically in the **word-processor**, illustrate it with clip-art or pupils' own artwork and print out revised versions for reference.
30	No Smoking!	Explore the use of fonts, styles, effects and colour to emphasise imperatives. Use a **word-processor** and the phrases on page 4 of the leaflet. Print out sample slogans using different fonts and styles and discuss design issues with the group or class.	Prepare a **template** in a **DTP** package with **image boxes** and **text frames** suitable for a leaflet. Pupils import the copy, lay up the pages and use suitable images to illustrate the leaflet.

Glossary of ICT terms

All teachers will need to understand and use the vocabulary associated with ICT and help children to use it appropriately and in context.

This list provides a broad summary of terms and acronyms which will be needed to provide support for children at Key Stage 2.

Address: the unique identifier for a web page. Typically an address takes the form http://www.repp.co.uk and should be entered into the address bar on the browser window. In this example, <repp.> is the name of the company owning the website, <co.> indicates that it is a company (others include <org.> for organisation, <gov.> for government, <sch.> for school, <ac.>for university etc.) and <uk> indicates the country. No country code usually indicates a US based website or a site, which regards itself as international.

Application: a piece of software, usually installed onto the computer or run over a network.

Attachment (see enclosure): a file sent with an e-mail message. An attachment may be text, graphics or sound. It may be helpful to imagine them as 'paper-clipped' to a file as a note may be attached to a paper document.

Authoring software (see presentation software): an application which enables the user to create documents using mixed media including text, still and moving images, and sound, with a means of moving between pages or screens. These packages may be used to produce presentations for use in the classroom or hall, as well as for creating web pages.

Back up: to make copies of documents or applications on another disk or tape as a safeguard against data loss. It is essential to keep regular back ups. Check the school policy with the ICT Co-ordinator.

Bookmark (see favourite): to store the address of a web page in a list in order to return to it during another session browsing the world wide web.

Browse: to move from page to page on a website or CD-ROM.

Browser software: an application which displays the pages of a website. The two major browser applications are Microsoft *Internet Explorer* and *Netscape Navigator*.

Clip art: images available commercially or as free collections distributed on disks, CD-ROM or the Internet, which may be incorporated into documents, multimedia presentations and websites.

Cut and paste: to move text or images from a document and place them in another part of the same document or into another document.

Database software: an application which enables the user to set up fields and records containing data, and to sort the data and display the information in a number of ways including graphs and charts.

Daylight projector: a piece of equipment which projects the display from a computer onto an external screen. The projectors may be wall- or ceiling-mounted or stand-alone portable devices.

DTP (desktop publishing) software: an application which enables the user to combine text and graphics, using templates for page-layout and styles. Text and graphics are typically placed in text or picture frames after having been originally created in word-processing, text-editing, painting or drawing packages.

Digital: information which is held in numerical form. Typically, in a computer, this is as a sequence of binary numbers.

Directory: a folder on the desktop which contains documents and sub-directories enabling users to organise their work, and find documents and applications easily. The directory system is often likened to a filing cabinet, with drawers, sub-divisions and folders.

Document: a single piece of work. A document may be in a word-processor, desktop publisher or database application. Each document must be saved with a unique filename.

Download: to save material such as text, images or software from another computer, the Internet or a network, and store it locally for future use on a hard disk or school network.

E-mail (electronic mail): a service provided on the Internet whereby electronic messages may be sent by one user to one or many other users throughout the world in a few minutes at minimal cost. In order to use e-mail, users will need to have e-mail software and a profile set up which includes a personal e-mail address.

Enclosure (see attachment): a file sent with an e-mail message. An enclosure may be text, graphics or sound.

Favourite (sometimes spelled favorite, see bookmark): to store the address of a web page in a list in order to return to it during another session browsing the world wide web.

Filename: the name used when saving a document as a file. It is important to use filenames that you and others will understand when sharing documents on a network or creating collections of digital resources.

Font: a set of type characters in the same style. A font will include different weights (bold, light, book) and different slants (italic, oblique). There are numerous fonts, some will be supplied with each application, others may be purchased or obtained from free collections.

Graphic: an image or picture.

Hyperlink: the electronic link to related information (text, graphics, sound, entire documents, whole pages or websites) which enables users to browse the Internet or a CD-ROM by making their own choices about routes through the material. The cursor will usually change from an arrow to, for example, a hand icon when it is over a hyperlink. Hyperlinks are often highlighted in some way such as underlining. Clicking on a hyperlink takes the user to the related page or website.

Image box (or image frame): the placeholder for a graphic, picture or image in a document.

Interactive whiteboard: a large, touch-sensitive board onto which an image of the computer desktop is projected. Users can interact with the projected image by drawing on the board with a stylus.

ISP (Internet service provider): the company providing Internet services such as e-mail and access to the world wide web for a school, organisation, business or household. Some ISPs do not charge for their services but may carry advertising. Check with your ICT Co-ordinator how to access Internet services from school.

Internet: the network of networks. Networks are formed by connecting computers. The Internet has been formed by connecting networks into a global network of networks. It provides a set of protocols which allow different networks to talk to each other, and services such as e-mail and the world wide web.

Intranet: a closed, private network or network of networks which uses the same protocols as the Internet and provides the same services such as e-mail.

LCD (liquid crystal display) panel: a flat screen display which can be used with a high powered overhead projector for presentations to groups.

Multimedia: the presentation of information through the use of more than one medium e.g. text, sound, images.

Network: formed by connecting computers in order to share files and applications. Networks are either peer-to-peer where any computer can talk to any other computer on the network or client/server where one computer holds all the files and applications and can be accessed by the client computers.

Optical character recognition (OCR) software: an application which enables a scanner to 'read' text and convert it into a digital form. Once saved, the text may be exported to a word-processor for editing.

PDF (portable document format): a proprietary document file format, for which a reader is freely available from Adobe, which has been designed to ensure that documents, particularly DTP documents retain all their formatting and typographic styles and effects when viewed on another computer.

Presentation software (see authoring software): an application which enables the user to create documents using mixed media including text, still and moving images and sound with a means of moving between pages or screens. These packages may be used to produce presentations for use in the classroom or hall.

Scanner: a piece of equipment which enables users to copy paper-based materials such as photographs or illustrations and save them in digital format. A scanner produces a bitmap image composed of pixels and works in a similar way to a photocopier. Many scanners include OCR software as standard.

Search engine: a service provided commercially on the Internet used to search for documents on the Internet. Users access the search engine from a web page on the providers website by entering key words. The service is usually free to the user and paid for by advertising.

Spell-checker: a function available in most word-processors and many other software applications which enables users to check spelling. It is important to remember that spell-checkers use a dictionary stored on the computer and will search it for logical matches. Users will need a certain basic level of spelling strategies to be able to make use of this facility. A spell-checker will not pick up mis-spelt words that are in the wrong context (for example, 'there' and 'their'). Some software has grammar checkers which teachers should consider using with care. Check what conventions are used. The problem with many grammar and spell-checker software is that is uses US English, although there may be opportunities to customise the dictionaries.

Stylesheet (see also template): 'blank' documents which may be saved to include margins, text styles, headers, footers, page-numbering, guidelines, image frames and text boxes amongst many other features which may be set up so that every page has a common format.

Table: a function available in some word-processors and spreadsheets to organise lists into tables. These may then be sorted according to various criteria such as date, alphabetical order, number etc. Tables should be used in preference to the <tab> key when putting lists into a word-processor.

Talking word-processor: speech output is available in some word-processing packages. The user may hear individual letters, words or complete sentences as they are keyed in, or on demand. This is very valuable as support for reading and writing activities.

Template: 'blank' documents which may be saved to include margins, text styles, headers, footers, page-numbering, guidelines, image frames and text boxes amongst many other features which may be set up so that every page has a common format. They are essential for use in desktop publishing packages and useful for word-processing. When writing more than a short paragraph, it is 'good practice' to set up styles for the entire document rather than make 'local' changes to, for example, centre and embolden a heading.

Text file: any file which contains plain text. When transferring text between different applications and computer platforms, it is advisable to select rich text format (RTF) from the save options.

Text frame (text box): the placeholder for text in a desktop publishing document.

Thesaurus: a function available in many word-processing applications for finding a synonym, an antonym, or related words for a selected word in the user's text.

Typing tutor: an application which trains users to touch type, typically using a structured 'drill' approach with on-screen copy to practise typing from.

Undo: a useful feature available in most software applications. Reverses the last action and may be used more than once in some applications to retrace a series of actions.

Website: a collection of pages published on the world wide web.

Word count: a function available in many word-processing applications for automatically counting the number of words, pages, characters and lines in a selected part of the document or the entire document.

Word-bank: a collection of words, customised by the user and stored in a word-processor. Many word-processors designed for the education market have word-bank facilities whereby selected groups of words and phrases may be saved and used to support writing. Check with the documentation in the program available for how to create and save word-banks.

Word-processing software: an application which enables users to manipulate text.

World wide web: an Internet service which provides information in the form of pages which can include text, images, video clips and sound. These are viewed using a web browser.